FINANCIAL FREEDOM,
LIFE FREEDOM

Escape the Earn-Spend Trap and
Design a Life That's Truly Yours

MARIE ORTEGA-STERLING

COPYRIGHT PAGE

Published by Supercritical Books
New York, United States
www.supercriticalbooks.com

Library of Congress Control Number: 2025920050
Paperback ISBN: 978-1-968988-00-5
Hardcover ISBN: 978-1-968988-02-9
eISBN: 978-1-968988-01-2

Cover design by: Ayoola Cheakina M.

Interior layout by: Vanessa Bruhm

Printed in the United States

First Edition 2025

For permissions, partnerships, or speaking inquiries, contact:
editorial@supercriticalbooks.com

Table of Contents

Reader's Preface

Your Life Was Never Meant to Be Trapped by a Paycheck

This book is for anyone who's ever felt the quiet dissonance between how life looks, and how it feels. You might be earning well. You might be doing "everything right." Yet somewhere beneath it all, there's a sense that something's missing. Maybe it's the slow burn of wasted potential, the kind that either simmers for years or suddenly erupts in a crisis. Or maybe it's the subtler constant ache of knowing you're not free, that your time belongs to someone else, and your deepest ambitions have been tucked away, drowned out by the relentlessness of the grind, and the never-ending busyness of life.

I wrote this book to help you come back to those dreams, and turn them into a life you can actually live. This book will help you build that freedom by guiding you to design a life where your values set the direction, and your expenses ride quietly in the backseat. A life where money becomes something steady and useful, something that helps you move toward freedom on your terms. A life where "success" is measured by what you're free to do, choose, and become, rather than solely by what you earn.

Across these chapters, you'll meet people like Marcus, who worked multiple jobs but still lived one crisis away from collapse; Jordan, who had money, status, and success, but couldn't shake the feeling.

That his life was drifting without meaning; and Lisa, a single mother whose spending was driven by exhaustion until she paused long enough to see the pattern. Their stories mirror our own through quiet realizations, difficult changes, and small, consistent choices that gradually move us toward something freer. Within their struggles and small victories, you'll find practical tools, mindset shifts, and deeply human reminders that change, however difficult, is possible. And that if we're willing to take conscious steps, repeated often, and grounded in our values, we can live freely.

The chapters move from rethinking money and spending habits to building resilience, creating purpose-driven budgets, embracing simple investing, and ultimately daring to dream again. It is a journey that includes financial clarity, emotional strength, and deeply personal growth.

If you remember nothing else, let this stay with you: you carry the power to begin. Every step forward starts with a clear decision. Change begins when you move with clarity, with purpose, and entirely on your terms, on your journey to financial freedom and life freedom.

With clarity and care,

Marie Ortega-Sterling

The Freedom Shift

Most people are taught how to build income. Fewer are taught how to build freedom.

From an early age, we're handed a template: get good grades, land a stable job, buy smart, save smart, move up. And there's wisdom in that. Earning matters. Progress matters. But somewhere along the way, the strategy becomes narrow. The focus sharpens so tightly on accumulation that we forget to ask: *To what end?*

Because for many, the better they perform, the tighter the grip on their time. The more they earn, the more their lives become structured around maintaining it. They hit the milestones others dream of; a decent salary, a solid apartment, some savings, and still feel strangely trapped.

This pattern shows up at every income level. It touches those struggling to get by, as well as high achievers with full calendars and empty weekends. Entrepreneurs with growing revenue and shrinking peace of mind. Young professionals sprinting toward a life they haven't yet defined.

If the system was designed to lead us toward freedom, why does it often leave us feeling exhausted, overextended, and unsure what all the effort is really for?

When Progress Still Feels Like Pressure

You can be doing everything right by following the rules, hitting the milestones and still feel like you're falling behind. Maybe your income has gone up over the years, but so have your obligations. Your calendar stays full, while your energy is drained. Or maybe you're just starting out, looking at rising costs and shrinking options, and wondering: how do I build a life that doesn't leave me burned out?

For many people, that moment comes quietly, with a slow realization: *I'm running hard, but I'm not getting free.*

That realization marks a turning point. It points to something honest, a sign that the strategy you were handed might not be built for the kind of life you actually want. Recognizing that is the beginning of real change.

The Story of Marcus King

Marcus King was 27 when everything finally caught up with him.

He'd grown up on the South Side of Chicago, in a neighborhood where you had to figure things out fast. His mother, Denise, worked long shifts as a nurse's aide, a job with low pay and no security. It left her tired all the time. His father had been gone for as long as he could remember. Marcus learned early how to step up. He walked his little sister to school, worked weekend shifts at the corner store, and handled problems quietly, because there wasn't anyone else to do it.

Teachers noticed his sharp mind. "He's going places," they'd say. But going places costs money. And when Denise injured her back on the job, college applications gave way to warehouse shifts and

Gas station hours. Now, Marcus had no choice but to work two jobs. At night he was unloading pallets, and during the day, he stood behind a cash register. Rent, groceries, bus passes, all of it consumed what he earned as fast as it came in.

Every payday hit the reset button. A high electric bill, a minor car issue, or a prescription could knock his whole month off course. He wasn't reckless. He wasn't lazy. He was just tired of survival mode.

So when he finally got a raise, a small one, but still something, he expected at least a little relief. But that's not what happened. Instead, the pressure and the stress grew worse. And the money? It disappeared, same as always. That's when it started to click. Maybe the problem wasn't only about what he earned. Maybe it had to do with how he'd been taught to use it. Or not taught, really, just expected to figure it out along the way.

On a break outside the warehouse, he leaned against the wall and told a friend, "I work all the time and I still don't have anything to show for it." His friend shrugged. "Yeah. That's how it goes, unless you start doing it differently." Something about that landed. And Marcus began to pay closer attention.

The Shift That Changed Everything

That conversation didn't solve anything. But it cracked something open. For the first time, Marcus began asking different questions. Why did he always feel broke, even after a raise? Why did payday offer a moment of relief, but never a sense of progress? Why did every step forward feel like it came with a hidden cost?

No one had ever really taught him how money worked. He had picked up bits and pieces, like most of us do, from family, school,

TV, work, and survival. And most of those messages were silent assumptions:

1. That the only way out was to earn more.
2. That budgeting was for people who already had plenty.
3. That building wealth was for someone else, particularly someone with fewer obstacles.

These beliefs kept him from succeeding, because they kept him from even trying. One day, he caught himself thinking through those ideas. They still sounded right to him, because they matched his lived reality. But for the first time, he did something different, he questioned whether they were complete. Whether, despite his obvious obstacles, there might be exceptions. And if there were, could any of them apply to him?

The moment he began to question those assumptions was the start of something bigger. Marcus didn't overhaul his life in a weekend. He didn't win the lottery or stumble into a high-paying job. He just started paying attention. To his spending, sure, but also to the stuff under it. The things he assumed without thinking. To the way he moved through each week. To the things he believed without ever saying out loud. To the advice he'd grown up around, and whether it was actually helping. He didn't know what to change yet. But he knew he wanted something different.

A New Way of Thinking

Marcus didn't have a master plan. He had questions. Small ones at first, mostly whispered late at night when the house was quiet and his feet still ached from work. He started listening more closely. This time, not to the usual loudest voices that had led him to where he was, but to those that made him stop and think. A podcast on the bus ride. A thread in a forum. A library book with no flashy cover, just stories of people who had done things differently. He wasn't looking for secrets. Mostly, he just wanted something that made sense.

He started noticing things. Like how easy it was to spend without thinking, letting money slip away through small habits. How payday came and went without anything really changing, just a bit of relief, but no real progress. How most of his choices came from pressure, from urgency, from reacting to one emergency or another.

So he started changing the way he moved through money, with small steps, taken on purpose. He tracked little things, a forgotten subscription here, a lunch habit there. He shifted priorities, setting a bit aside up front, even when it felt like there wasn't much to work with. And over time, the way he saw himself started to shift. He was beginning to feel a sense of control, moving beyond mere survival.

The difference showed up in more than just how he felt. As Marcus kept going, the numbers started to move too. His bank balance started to grow, mainly because money wasn't disappearing without direction. He managed to build a bit of savings, which barely existed before, and now it gave him a bit of breathing room. Even his debt, which had always felt too heavy to move, started to shrink. And with that, new choices began to appear. At the end of six months, things looked different. He could say no to toxic extra shifts. He could plan instead of scrambling every time something went wrong. He didn't feel rich. But he didn't feel stuck anymore either. And that made all the difference.

This was a financial shift born from a mindset shift, a decision to treat money as something to shape, not merely to earn; it was neither a miracle nor a breakthrough. And that's what this book is here to offer you. You won't find hacks or hustle scripts. What you'll find are quiet revolutions, the kind that begin with small wins, slowly build into financial stability, and eventually give you the freedom to live in a way that once felt out of reach, especially when all you've known is working just to stay afloat.

You'll learn how to use your income with more intention, so that money becomes something you can manage, something that supports the life you actually want. It's about finding ways to buy back your time, beginning with small, steady changes that gradually open up your day. It's about saying yes to what matters most, and learning how to say no without guilt. That kind of freedom grows when you begin to look at what you already have a little differently. Because financial freedom isn't about chasing more, it's about needing less, using what you've got with care, and building the kind of stability that lets you walk away when you need to, change direction when it matters, and rest without anxiety.

And it begins with one honest question about your life as it is, right now: *What does freedom really mean to you?*

CHAPTER 1

The Power of Choice

WHY FINANCIAL FREEDOM IS REALLY ABOUT CHOICE

True financial independence is more than it seems on the surface. It's often seen as having plenty of money or living in comfort, but that definition misses the deeper point. At its core, it's about having the power to shape your life on your terms, and that power includes more than just money or the comfort it brings. It means gaining the freedom to make meaningful choices, free from the influence of obligation, fear, or habit.

What actually matters to you? Is it spending more time with your family? Traveling without having to ask for time off? Doing work that feels aligned with your values? Or simply sleeping well at night because you know you're secure?

These answers are deeply personal. Yet many people never take the time to ask these questions let alone answer them with honesty. Instead, they get swept into a rhythm of earning, spending, saving, and striving. They live a life of motion without direction, without clarity, and without ever pausing long enough to ask: *What am I truly building this life for?*

That was exactly the case for Jordan Ellis.

Jordan was 29 and living in Seattle, with a tech job that paid well and a career path that looked impressive from the outside. He had the modern markers of success: a one-bedroom loft with skyline views, a sleek electric car, and a résumé full of fast promotions and glowing reviews. People often said he was "killing it." But inside, Jordan felt strangely adrift.

He couldn't remember the last time he had taken a deep breath without checking his calendar. Most of his meals were from takeout containers eaten at his desk. He hadn't seen his childhood friends in months. And though he was saving money, he had no real sense of what he was saving for.

One night, after another long 14-hour workday, Jordan came home, dropped his bag by the door, and sank onto his couch in silence, numb and exhausted. He unlocked his phone and began scrolling through job listings out of habit, hoping a new job might offer a way out even though he didn't truly need one.

That's when the realization hit. "I've spent years building this life," he thought. "But I never stopped to ask if it's the life I actually want."

That moment of clarity quiet and undeniable lingered in his chest with a kind of stillness that demanded attention. As with Marcus King, it started the same way for Jordan: with the simple act of paying attention.

Jordan paused long enough to notice the emptiness beneath his achievements. He had been chasing success without ever defining it for himself. And like many people, he had assumed that more money, more status, and more productivity would eventually lead to happiness.

But it hadn't because without a clear personal definition of success, "more" will never feel like enough.

That insight became his turning point. As he numbly scrolled through job listings, seeking an undefined "way out," a stark realization emerged: none of them offered what he truly craved. What he truly needed was a different life.

He began to see that all his external achievements meant little without an internal compass. He didn't quit his job the next day or throw away his belongings, but he started asking better questions. He began to reconsider how he used his time, how he spent his money, and what kind of life he was actually building.

Financial independence, for him, became a matter of clarity and intention a daily practice of making decisions that reflected his true priorities. It meant learning to live in alignment with what mattered most and grounding that alignment in a clear understanding of his values.

Without that foundation, even a financially successful life can feel adrift and lacking in meaning.

THE PROBLEM: LIVING WITHOUT DEFINED CORE VALUES

Many people drift through life without a clear sense of what they stand for. Their choices are influenced by immediate pressures, routine, or what others expect of them, rather than being rooted in deliberate, deeply held core values.

Society only makes it harder, endlessly promoting a narrow ideal of achievement: the giant house, the expensive car, the prestigious job title. These messages are everywhere, subtly telling us that

Wealth equals worth. Yet we rarely pause to ask the deeper question: What actually makes me feel fulfilled?

That was the heart of Jordan's realization. On the surface, he had everything: salary, status, lifestyle. But underneath, he felt aimless worn down by a life he never consciously chose. His story shows what happens when success is defined by external standards rather than internal values. He had more than enough but didn't know why.

Lisa's story, which you're about to encounter, reveals a quieter but equally powerful truth: even when we're focused on surviving, the absence of clear values still shapes our lives just in subtler, harder-to-see ways. While Jordan's life was full on the surface and empty underneath, Lisa's was stretched thin from the start.

He struggled to find meaning in his success; she struggled to find breathing room in her survival. But both stories point to the same truth: without clear values to guide us, we end up making choices that slowly wear us down even when they feel necessary at the time.

That's exactly where Lisa Carter found herself.

At 34, Lisa was a single mom raising two kids in Columbus, Ohio. Her world revolved around meeting daily needs: getting the kids to school, clocking in for her shift at the pharmacy, covering rent and daycare, squeezing in grocery runs between responsibilities. Her goals were simple and noble: keep her kids safe, keep the lights on, and try to save a little when she could.

But under the surface, stress was constant. A car breakdown could unravel her entire month. A missed paycheck would mean falling behind. She told herself she was doing okay, because everything was technically covered, until it wasn't.

Her days were long, her energy drained, and despite her best efforts, she rarely felt ahead. To cope, she leaned on small comforts: takeout after a long shift, quick retail therapy at discount stores, little conveniences that made life feel manageable for a moment. But even as she spent, she felt a lingering guilt. The relief never lasted.

Her wake-up call came late one evening. She was sitting at the kitchen table with a pile of bank statements spread out in front of her. Her kids were finally asleep. The house was quiet. And as she looked over her spending from the past three months, realization began to form, not just about the numbers, but about the pattern beneath them. Her financial decisions weren't supporting the life she wanted to build. They weren't creating more security. They weren't buying her more time with her children. They weren't rooted in any long-term vision at all.

That was the turning point, understanding where the stress came from. Her money wasn't being guided by anything clear. It was reacting to exhaustion, emotion, and urgency. She saw it clearly, she was surviving on autopilot. That night, she made a quiet but powerful decision: no more default choices. No more going through the motions.

She began asking herself two questions before every purchase, no matter how small:

- *Is this moving me closer to the life I want for my family?*
- *Does this bring me peace, or just temporary comfort?*

It wasn't easy at first. The habits ran deep. But within weeks, she noticed a shift. She wasn't reacting to her financial stress anymore, she was responding with intention. She started trimming the unnecessary, prioritizing her values, and finding new ways to make her money reflect what mattered most: stability, time with her kids, and peace of mind.

For the first time, she didn't feel like she was just working to stay afloat. She felt like she was steering her life with clarity. That's when she truly understood: financial independence is about how closely your decisions align with your deepest values, more than just how much you earn. And once you define those values, everything starts to change.

WHAT DO YOU TRULY CARE ABOUT?

Identifying Your Core Values

At the heart of financial freedom lies a simple yet profound question one that most people, like Marcus, Jordan, and Lisa, never thought to slow down to ask: What do I truly care about?

Your core values are more than abstract ideals or statements hung on a corporate office wall or hidden in the "About Us" tab of a website. They are, in essence, personal operating systems that influence how you spend, how you save, and how you make decisions whether you realize it or not.

The challenge is that many of us adopt our values unconsciously from the world around us, shaped by culture, advertising, and expectations we've never questioned. But when your financial life begins to reflect values you've chosen deliberately, things feel more grounded. And when it doesn't, even success can feel strangely hollow.

Jason Patel experienced this firsthand. As a corporate lawyer in New York, he earned more than he ever imagined. He had the job, the apartment, the status. From the outside, it looked like he had won.

But day after day, his time didn't feel like his own: late nights, constant pressure, and a schedule that left no room for the things that made life feel human. One weekend, during his cousin's graduation, he found himself replying to client emails in the middle of the ceremony. That night, back in his hotel room, he sat in silence and asked a question he had never let himself consider:

If financial success doesn't give me more freedom over how I spend my days, what is it really worth?

That moment stayed with him. It didn't lead to an overnight change, and he didn't leave his job the next day. But something took root. He began asking better questions the kind that don't go away. He made a quiet list of what mattered most: time with people he cared about, space for his health, a calmer rhythm to his days. Then, little by little, he started adjusting the way he earned, spent, and planned.

Some changes came naturally. Others resisted. The pull of old habits was strong. But over time, his life began to feel less reactive and more deliberate less like something to keep up with, and more like something he was truly shaping.

Jason's story shows that clarity is only the beginning. Real freedom requires intentional redesign: translating values into daily decisions, not just lofty ideals. Because true financial independence is about how honestly your money reflects what matters to you. And when you start there, everything begins to shift.

THE DANGER OF LIVING ON AUTOPILOT

Many people move through life following a familiar script: work hard, spend to keep up, save when possible, and hope to retire someday. But few pause to ask whether that path truly reflects their deepest hopes or values.

Living on autopilot is one of the greatest hidden risks to a meaningful life. It leads to choices shaped not by personal clarity but by habit and outside pressure by what others expect, what society praises, and what advertising suggests we need.

Without realizing it, you can build a life that looks successful but feels deeply disconnected.

Signs You're Living on Autopilot

Autopilot doesn't always show up as a crisis. Often, it reveals itself through quiet patterns that shape your days without your awareness. You might stay in a job that doesn't energize you simply because it feels stable. You might spend money in ways that impress others but don't reflect what truly matters to you. Or you might feel a constant, low-level anxiety around money not because you're careless, but because you've never clearly defined how much is enough for the life you actually want.

These are signs of a life shaped by default rather than design.

It's the same realization that Jordan, Lisa, and Jason each had to face.

Jordan had wealth but lacked direction. His days were full, but his sense of purpose was missing. Lisa knew what mattered to her children, stability, peace but her habits weren't aligned with those values. And Jason had everything success was supposed to offer status, income, recognition but no control over how he spent his time.

Each of them reached a quiet turning point: a moment when the cost of autopilot living became impossible to ignore. They saw that without conscious direction, it's possible to build a life that meets expectations but forgets the person living it.

Waking up isn't easy. But it's where freedom begins.

TRY THIS:

Imagine your ideal ordinary day not a vacation, but a day that feels deeply right to you. Where are you? What time do you wake up? Who are you with, and what are you doing? What does your work, your pace, your environment feel like?

Now compare that vision to your current daily reality. What's different? What's missing? What would need to shift to bring you even one step closer?

This simple exercise can reveal the quiet gap between the life you're living and the one you long for. And that clarity is often where intentional change begins.

CREATING YOUR PERSONAL DEFINITION OF SUCCESS

Success isn't one-size-fits-all. For some, it means reaching financial independence by 40. For others, it's doing meaningful work with flexibility or having the freedom to spend more time with family. The key is defining success on your terms and giving yourself permission to pursue what truly matters to you, not what others expect.

Start by asking: *What does success feel like to me?*

It's easy to chase external milestones, but real success runs deeper. Does it feel like peace? Excitement? Purpose? Take time to explore this on an emotional level. Because if success doesn't feel right on the inside, it won't feel like success at all.

Then ask: *How does money fit into that picture?*

Think of money as a tool not the goal. It's powerful when used with intention, but it's not the destination. Once you're clear on what success means to you, ask how money can support that vision. If success means freedom to travel, for example, you might prioritize experiences over possessions.

And finally: *Let it evolve.*

Your definition of success will change over time and that's not failure; it's growth. Staying true to your values means being willing to revisit them, to shift your goals as your life changes.

True success isn't static. It's a reflection of who you are and what matters most, at every stage of your life.

TRY THIS:
Craft a simple sentence that captures what a fulfilling life looks like for you. Don't worry about making it perfect. This is for you, to serve as a personal compass to help keep your decisions aligned with what truly matters.

Example: *Success to me is having the freedom to work on projects I care about while spending time with people I love.*

Write yours. Keep it somewhere visible. Let it anchor your choices, and revisit it often, as your life changes, so should your definition.

ALIGNING YOUR FINANCIAL GOALS WITH YOUR LIFE VISION

By now, you've seen how this plays out in real lives Jordan, Lisa, and Jason each reached a moment when the old script stopped working, and a deeper clarity took hold. They didn't just want more money. They wanted a life that felt true one where their time, spending, and decisions flowed from what they genuinely valued.

That's what *alignment* really means. It's not about sacrificing ambition or comfort it's about ensuring your financial goals serve the life you actually want. When your values come into focus, money stops being a source of confusion or pressure. It becomes a tool for building something meaningful, day by day.

That shift isn't always easy especially when money, status, or momentum are tied to your current path. But it's possible.

Across industries, an increasing number of people are choosing alignment over accumulation. In Silicon Valley, for instance, some engineers and executives have walked away from peak earnings and stock options not because they failed, but because they redefined success. They chose time with their kids, creative freedom, or simply a slower, saner pace.

So now, the question shifts to you:

What kind of life are you shaping and is your money helping you shape it?

STEPS TO ALIGN MONEY WITH YOUR VALUES

Examine your spending with fresh eyes.

Take a moment to really look at where your money has been going not with guilt, but with curiosity. What patterns do you notice? Are you consistently investing in things that bring real joy, rest, or meaning? Or are there habits that have crept in unnoticed subscriptions you've forgotten, purchases made out of convenience, or spending that numbs more than it nourishes? This isn't about perfection. It's about waking up to your own financial story and gently asking whether it reflects the life you want to live. Honesty here is the beginning of alignment.

Experience the freedom of letting go.

Letting go of expenses that don't reflect your values isn't about restriction it's about making room. Every time you say no to something that doesn't matter, you're saying yes to something that does. That might be more time, less stress, or the ability to redirect money toward the parts of your life that truly need it. Canceling a forgotten service, resisting an impulse buy, or choosing a simpler path isn't just good budgeting it's a quiet act of reclaiming power.

Save and invest with intention.

Money feels different when it has a destination that matters to you. When you're clear about what you're building whether it's a few months of breathing room, a sabbatical, a creative project, or an early retirement, it becomes easier to make trade-offs with confidence. You're not just saving *"because you should"*; you're saving to move closer to a life that feels like yours. This clarity gives purpose to your effort and turns financial discipline into forward motion.

TRY THIS: REVISIT YOUR LAST 10 PURCHASES

Open your bank or credit card statement and take a quiet moment to review your last ten transactions not to judge yourself, but to learn. Which of those purchases still feels good, like they supported something that matters to you? Which ones felt fleeting, automatic, or out of sync with the life you want to build?

This isn't about guilt. It's about noticing. Ask yourself: If I could go back, *what would I do differently*? What would I gladly repeat? Small as it may seem, this kind of reflection can begin to shift the way you spend toward more intention, more meaning, and more alignment between your money and your values.

FINAL CHALLENGE: THE 30-DAY CLARITY EXPERIMENT

For the next 30 days, challenge yourself to live with full financial awareness and intention. Each day, commit to these three small but powerful actions:

Track every expense and reflect.

After each purchase, pause and ask yourself: Does this align with my values? Keep a daily log. Over time, patterns will emerge. Some affirming, others eye-opening. This simple practice can help you shift from unconscious spending to intentional choice.

Make one intentional financial decision each day.

It could be skipping a small expense you don't truly value, redirecting money toward a priority, or spending generously on something that brings real joy or peace. These daily choices build momentum, rewiring your habits from the inside out.

Write down one long-term goal that reflects your personal version of success.

Not a goal rooted in what you think you should want, but one that feels deeply yours. Keep it somewhere visible. Let it anchor your efforts, guiding your daily decisions and reminding you what all this awareness is for.

Your Goal: To gain clear, honest insight into how your financial life aligns with your values and where it quietly drifts away from them. Over these 30 days, you're not aiming for perfection, but for awareness the kind of awareness that sharpens your sense of what matters most and helps you move forward with intention.

You might be surprised how much can shift just by paying attention. Small clarity has a way of reshaping big decisions.

CLOSING THOUGHTS: YOU GET TO CHOOSE

Financial freedom isn't about having more it's about having control over your choices. It's the ability to make decisions that reflect your values and priorities, instead of being pulled by pressure, comparison, or convention. When you define what truly matters to you, money becomes a tool and a way to build a life that feels rich in all the ways that count.

The path forward starts with clarity. It means defining your values as the foundation for freedom. It means living with intention, choosing goals and actions that align with who you are and what you care about. And it means using money as it was meant to be used: as a means to support your vision of success and fulfillment not a measure of it.

YOUR NEXT STEP:

Make one small decision today that moves you closer to the life you want whether it's setting a clear financial goal, letting go of an expense that no longer serves you, or simply taking a few quiet minutes to reflect on your values.

What's next?

In Chapter 2, we'll explore how small, consistent actions lead to lasting transformation. You'll learn how to build habits that support your financial goals and shape a life that feels abundant, grounded, and truly free.

Tiny Changes, Big Results: The Compound Effect of Small Wins

THE MYTH OF OVERNIGHT SUCCESS

In a world built on speed, the idea of overnight success is powerfully seductive. We're surrounded by headlines about lottery winners who wake up millionaires, tech entrepreneurs who build billion-dollar apps in their twenties, influencers who go viral and suddenly quit their jobs to live on sponsorship deals. These stories get repeated, shared, and amplified because they offer something we're all wired to crave: the hope of immediate transformation.

The message is subtle but constant: one big break can change everything. It's the dream of waking up tomorrow in a different life the belief that with the right spark, luck, timing, or genius, you can leap from struggle to success without the messy in-between.

And yet, for most people, this version of success remains just out of reach. Not because they're not smart enough or ambitious enough, but because the path they're on looks very different from the glamorous stories they see. It's slower, less dramatic, and sometimes invisible, but also more real. Because the truth is, lasting success almost never comes in a single flash. It's built through small, deliberate actions repeated consistently over time not the result of one grand decision or stroke of luck. And as Marcus King was about to learn, that truth can be frustrating until it becomes freeing.

Marcus Tries to Change Everything

It had been almost a month since Marcus started paying attention. The conversation with his friend outside the warehouse had stayed with him like a pebble in his shoe subtle but impossible to ignore. For the first time in years, he had started looking at his money differently. Watching it move. Noticing what drained him. Realizing that half his spending came from habit, not intention.

But his story didn't unfold in a straight line. Marcus's path had a messy middle, and it's one many of us will recognize.

It began when his shifts changed. The warehouse was rotating teams, and for once, Marcus had three days off in a row. It felt like a window opening. He told himself this was the moment to get things right. He sat at his kitchen table with a notepad, a calculator, and a rising sense of urgency. He wrote a strict budget. Canceled every subscription. Swore off takeout. Vowed to save half his income. Downloaded three budgeting apps. Created daily reminders. Watched hours of YouTube advice.

"This time, I'm going all in," he said out loud. And for a few days, it worked. He felt focused. Disciplined. In control. And quite frankly, it looked that way to anyone watching.

But within two weeks, the cracks began to show. Skipping small comforts left him tired. His ultra-lean budget felt punishing. He stopped responding to friends, afraid any social event would wreck his plan. When his car needed a minor repair, the entire system collapsed.

By the end of the month, he wasn't tracking anything at all. He felt like he had failed again. The familiar frustration crept in. Maybe he wasn't cut out for this. Maybe financial control was just for people with higher incomes, more structure, or better luck.

But then he paused. For once, he didn't just walk away from the failure. He sat with it.

And that, without him fully realizing it, was the real turning point.

Maybe You've Been There Too

Maybe your story doesn't look exactly like Marcus's, but chances are, you've felt something similar. Maybe it was after a tough financial month, and you promised yourself you'd reset. Maybe it was a new year, a Monday morning, or a burst of motivation after watching a TED talk or reading a finance blog. You felt clear, ready, and determined. This time would be different. So you set ambitious goals. You made a plan. You cut things out. You swore off old habits. And then, life happened. You got tired. An unexpected bill showed up. Or maybe you just had a bad day and needed comfort more than discipline. And slowly, the big plan unraveled. Not because you were weak, but because it was too much, too fast.

I've been there too.

I remember a few years ago, I decided to overhaul everything in one weekend—my finances, my diet, my screen time. I downloaded three tracking apps, built a complicated spreadsheet, and spent hours building routines I was sure I'd follow forever. By

Wednesday, I was overwhelmed. By Friday, I was back to takeout and untracked spending. It wasn't that I lacked motivation. I was just trying to change in a way that wasn't built to last.

That's the trap of the "all-or-nothing" mindset. It feels productive in the moment, but it often leads to burnout, not progress.

That experience taught me something I've never forgotten:

Big change is almost always a trap. It excites you, then exhausts you.

But small change, quiet, repeatable, unglamorous, that's what actually sticks. And that's what makes compounding so powerful.

THE POWER OF COMPOUNDING: A 1% IMPROVEMENT EVERY DAY

One of the most powerful forces in your financial life is also one of the quietest. You won't see it in a single day or week, but over time, it changes everything. It's the effect of small improvements, repeated consistently.

If you improve by just 1% each day not perfectly, just steadily you'll be nearly 38 times better than where you started by the end of the year.

Let things slip by 1% each day, and you'll drift toward zero. That's the quiet math of momentum.

This idea, recently popularized by James Clear in *Atomic Habits*, reveals a truth that's easy to forget:

Big wins don't come from massive efforts. They come from small steps, done often.

Because compounding doesn't reward intensity, it rewards consistency.

And here's the catch: it works in both directions. Whether you're moving toward clarity or drifting away from it, compounding is always at work.

Emily's Story: The Reverse Compound Effect

Emily Rhodes had tripled her income over the last five years. She had earned every step of it switching companies, negotiating better offers, and earning certifications on weekends. By most standards, she was doing well. With each raise, she felt a mix of pride and relief. She could finally breathe a little.

But with every increase, something else had quietly followed.

A slightly newer car. A roomier apartment. Nicer restaurants. A few more streaming services. A couple of weekend getaways that turned into a habit. Nothing felt excessive. In fact, most of it felt like a reward a natural reflection of how far she'd come.

It wasn't until one evening, scanning through her spending history out of curiosity, that she saw the pattern clearly. Her income had gone up. But so had everything else.

The gap she thought she was building the margin that was supposed to give her freedom had quietly disappeared. The more she earned, the more her life expanded to match it. The progress she'd worked so hard for had been quietly absorbed by routine.

It wasn't the result of impulsive spending. It was the result of small, unconscious choices made on autopilot.

That's the reverse compound effect: small, unexamined choices accumulating in the background, pulling you further from the security or flexibility you thought you were building.

The Lesson: Lifestyle Inflation

Lifestyle inflation is the silent erosion of financial progress. It happens when your spending rises alongside your income often without conscious decisions. The danger isn't in a single big purchase. It's in the steady accumulation of small upgrades that feel normal, even deserved, but slowly consume the margin you could be using to build security, freedom, or long-term wealth.

For Emily, the most unsettling part wasn't any single purchase it was what all the small upgrades had added up to: a more expensive life that looked better on the outside but left her just as financially stretched as before. She realized she hadn't been standing still she had been slowly drifting backward. That's the thing about compounding: it doesn't care whether your habits are helpful or harmful. It just multiplies the direction you're already moving in.

THE POWER OF SMALL WINS: BIG DOORS SWING ON SMALL HINGES

The idea that small actions lead to big results isn't groundbreaking, but it's easy to ignore the hype especially in a world that celebrates dramatic overhauls and overnight success.

Consider two people:

- Person A quietly saves $5 every working day weekdays only, with holidays off. No fanfare. Just consistency.
- Person B thinks saving $5 a day is pointless too small to matter.

After one year:

1. Person A has saved around $1,240.
2. Person B has saved nothing.

Now stretch that out over ten years:

- Person A has over $12,000 *before* any interest or investment returns.
- Person B still has nothing.

Add even a modest 7% annual return, and the gap widens significantly.

It's easy to dismiss small habits as insignificant. But over time, the gap between action and inaction becomes enormous. That's the quiet math of momentum. The real difference doesn't come from dramatic moves it comes from steady, old-fashioned repetition. That's exactly what changed David Martinez's perspective.

David's Wake-Up Call

It was a wet Thursday evening, and David was late for dinner. He stepped into the small Thai restaurant, brushing rain from his jacket. Across the table, his friend Matt was already halfway through a plate of pad thai.

They hadn't seen each other in a while. The conversation drifted from work to money.

"I've been thinking about saving again," David said. "But honestly, fifty bucks a month just feels like a joke." Matt raised an eyebrow. "I've been doing that every month for years."

David gave a short laugh. "Okay, but what's that add up to like a couple grand?" Matt didn't argue. He just opened his phone, tapped a few times, and slid it across the table. The screen showed a balance: $12,000+.

David stared. His smile faded not from jealousy, but because the math had just cracked through his story. On the walk home, rain soaking through his hoodie, David couldn't stop thinking about it. Ten years. Fifty bucks. No secret. Just time.

The next morning, he opened his investment account. Just fifty dollars and a decision to stop waiting. Because that's the thing about small habits: they seem easy to dismiss... until they prove you wrong.

Most people think, *"Ten bucks won't change my life."*

But $10 per working day, invested at 7% for 20 years, grows to over $100,000. That's what Emily never saw coming. And what David only believed once the math spoke for itself. Because the compound effect begins with consistency. And when you add even a modest increase in intensity, it accelerates dramatically Save $40 per working day, and in those same 20 years? You'd have over $400,000.

EXERCISE: IDENTIFY YOUR "TINY WIN" AREAS

To get started, choose one area to focus on:

1. **Spending**: Scan your recent transactions and choose one low-value habit you can pause. Maybe it's a delivery service you barely use or an app you forgot you subscribed to. Cancel it and reassign that money toward something you *actually* care about.

2. **Saving:** Automate even small amounts. It doesn't have to be hundreds, start with what feels doable. Set up a recurring transfer, even if it's just $10 every Friday. Over time, you'll build the habit without having to think about it, and the growing balance will start to reflect the momentum you've built.

3. **Investing:** Don't wait until you feel "ready." Start with whatever you can afford, $25, $50, even less. The goal isn't to time the market perfectly. It's to participate. Use a simple index fund or a robo-advisor if you're unsure where to begin. You're not just building wealth, you're building confidence.

4. **Learning:** Spend five minutes a day getting smarter with money. That could be one short article, a few pages of a book, or even a podcast episode on your commute. These days, you can also ask an AI to break down a financial concept for you like compound interest or index funds, at your own pace. Think of it as having a private tutor, always on standby. The point is to keep learning forward, letting the learnings accumulate.

HOW TO MAKE SMALL WINS AUTOMATIC

One of the simplest ways to make small wins stick is to remove the need for willpower altogether. That's where automation comes in. When you automate your savings or investment contributions, no matter how small, you don't have to remember, decide, or motivate yourself each time. It just happens quietly, consistently, in the background while you get on with your life.

Another method is what some call "habit stacking." Instead of trying to carve out time and space for a brand-new routine, attach it to something you already do. Do you check your phone each morning? Make it a trigger to glance at your spending from yesterday. Do you brew a cup of tea in the evening? Use that moment to move a little money to savings. The goal isn't to add complexity, it's to fit the habit into your day like a note in your pocket. Something that stays with you, almost unnoticed, but slowly changing things.

And then there's this: if an action takes almost no time, just a moment of effort, do it now. Don't put off what could quietly push things forward. Often, it's the smallest tasks we delay the longest: opening a new savings account, canceling a subscription we forgot about, or tweaking a setting that's been off for months. These aren't big moves, but they start a shift a light push that gets the wheel turning again.

TRY THIS:

Log into your banking app and schedule a small recurring transfer, whatever amount feels light and doable. You'll be surprised how quickly these quiet choices begin to shape your future.

THE DANGER OF SMALL BAD HABITS

The Flip Side of Compounding

Just as good habits quietly build your future, bad ones quietly wear it down, not all at once, just a little, over and over. That's what makes them dangerous: they rarely seem urgent enough to stop.

Emily's story showed that clearly. No single expense was the issue, but her direction day by day was slipping. The compound effect doesn't care which way you're headed. It just multiplies what you repeat.

So ask yourself: What's one small habit, barely noticeable, that might be working against you? Not to feel guilty, but to see it. Because once you notice the drift, you can shift. And that shift doesn't have to be dramatic. It just has to begin now.

FINAL CHALLENGE: THE 30-DAY SMALL WINS EXPERIMENT

Pick one small financial habit. Just one. Then stick with it for 30 days.

Here are a few to try:

- Save $1 a day.
- Round up your purchases and invest the difference.
- Read one page of a financial book each day.
- Check your accounts once a week, calmly, without judgment.

Your goal: Don't overhaul your life. Just prove to yourself that small wins add up.

By the end of the month, you'll see something shift. Maybe it's your savings balance. Maybe it's how you think about money. Either way, you'll have real proof: progress doesn't need to be dramatic to be real.

CLOSING THOUGHTS: START SMALL, STAY CONSISTENT

Every meaningful financial change begins with something small an action so ordinary it's easy to overlook. But done consistently, those small steps begin to change the course of your future. You don't need to overhaul everything. You just need to begin. Automate a transfer. Pause before a purchase. Read a single page. Let momentum build through repetition, not pressure.

Start now not because it's urgent, but because it's easy to wait. Small wins become big shifts. All they need is time and your effort.

What's Next?

In Chapter 3, we'll shift from understanding how small actions grow to building a savings-first mindset, one that makes saving effortless instead of a struggle. You'll learn how to prioritize saving, automate your finances, and create a system that works for you.

Building a Savings Mindset: Make Saving Effortless

INTRODUCTION: WHY MOST PEOPLE STRUGGLE TO SAVE

Saving money is one of those universal goals that everyone agrees is important, yet so many of us find it incredibly challenging. It's often framed as a struggle, as something difficult even restrictive. Especially when the month feels longer than the money. For many, it's not a lack of desire that holds them back. It's the sense that saving only works after everything else has been paid. And by then, there's rarely anything left.

Sophia Ramirez never thought she had a problem with saving. She wasn't reckless with money. She paid her bills on time. She didn't chase luxury or live beyond her means. On paper, she was responsible. But her savings account always told a different story: flatlined, month after month.

It hit her one evening in early spring. She was sitting by the window of her apartment, sunlight spilling across the hardwood floor, her laptop open with a half-finished spreadsheet and two tabs of online shopping open in the background. Rent had just gone out. Groceries, utilities, a friend's birthday gift it all added up, again.

She stared at the leftover balance in her checking account, the number smaller than she expected, smaller than she wanted. Again.

"I'll save more next month," she said to herself. But that month never seemed to come. Saving, it turned out, wasn't about effort or intention. It was about timing. And Sophia had been trying to save at the end, when everything else had already taken its bite. What finally shifted her mindset wasn't some dramatic breakthrough. It was a quiet realization: if saving weren't the first move, it would always be the leftover move.

But here's the real surprise: for most people, the biggest barrier to saving usually isn't their income. It's the mindset they bring to it, and the system they rely on. Most people, like Sophia, treat saving as an afterthought something done only if money remains, perceiving it as a sacrifice, restriction, or delay of joy. So we put it off. "I'll start saving when I earn more," we tell ourselves. But when that day comes, the pattern stays the same. The more money we earn, the more we spend, and the result stays the same.

What changes everything is a shift in our habits and in how we think about saving. When we see it as something that comes first, not last, everything begins to realign.

That's what this chapter is about. Not budgeting harder, or saying no to everything fun, but rewiring how you approach saving so it becomes automatic, sustainable, and even satisfying. By the end, you'll have the tools to make saving feel less like a chore and more like a quiet form of freedom you carry with you.

WHY TRADITIONAL BUDGETING FAILS

Let's start by addressing the elephant in the room: traditional budgeting. Most people try to save by tracking every expense and trimming their spending month after month. On paper, it makes sense. In practice, it rarely sticks. Here's why:

It relies on willpower.

Traditional budgeting expects you to say "no" to dozens of temptations each week, sometimes each day. It turns every purchase into a moral decision not just *can I afford this?* But *should I want this?* Over time, that constant judgment wears you down. Not because you're weak, but because you're human. Without a system to lean on, even the best intentions eventually give way to stress, emotion, or just a hard day.

It feels restrictive.

When saving always starts with "no," it quickly begins to feel like punishment. Budgeting can start to feel less like planning and more like self-denial on repeat. You're not just trying to spend less you're constantly negotiating with yourself. *Do I need this? Can I justify that?* Eventually, the process wears you down, not just financially, but mentally too. That's when you start avoiding your budget altogether not because you don't care, but because it feels like a constant reminder that you're falling short.

Life happens.

Even the most carefully planned budget can be undone by the unexpected: a surprise car repair, a medical bill, a last-minute gift for a friend's birthday. These aren't failures, they're life. But when your system relies on everything going exactly right, even one disruption can feel like a collapse. And that feeling? It's often enough to make people throw out the whole plan not because they're careless, but because their budget didn't leave space for being human.

It misaligns with what matters.

Most budgets focus on numbers what goes where, and what gets cut. But they rarely ask what matters to you. And when your spending plan ignores your values, it starts to feel like deprivation for no good reason. You cut out dinners with friends, skip little joys, and tell yourself it's for the best. But if you're not clear on what you're actually building toward, it just feels like a loss. Saving should help you protect what makes life meaningful.

That's exactly what Marcus King realized.

Back in Chapter 2, we watched him attempt an overnight transformation. He canceled subscriptions, swore off takeout, and vowed to save half his income. It collapsed within weeks.

Later, he told himself he just needed more structure. So he tried a traditional budget instead. He downloaded new apps, tracked every transaction, and stuck to a detailed plan. And for a little while, it worked. But slowly, the cracks returned.

Every purchase became a negotiation. Every moment of joy felt like something he had to justify. He found himself saying no to things he valued, unsure what he was even saying yes to.

One unexpected expense, his sister's birthday dinner, threw the entire plan off course. It didn't ruin him financially, but the guilt hit hard. The plan unraveled. He realized then that for saving to work long-term, it had to be easy and automatic, not a constant struggle. It had to fit into life, not fight against it.

THE PSYCHOLOGY OF SAVING – HOW TO TRICK YOUR BRAIN

Saving often feels like a rational decision, fighting an emotional reflex. That's because your brain is wired to prioritize immediate rewards over future ones. It's not a failure of discipline; it's biology. Spending gives you something now. Saving asks you to wait. That mismatch creates friction.

But here's the good news: you can work with your brain, not against it. With a few subtle adjustments, you can make saving feel just as rewarding as spending, sometimes even more.

Turn Saving Into a Game

Sophia didn't think of herself as impulsive. But every so often, a scroll through online shops would turn into a checkout. A little reward, a moment of escape. It wasn't about the stuff; it was about the mood, a way of breaking monotony.

That changed when she discovered a different kind of reward: turning saving itself into a game. She started with one rule: no purchases for 72 hours unless necessary. Then she stretched it. She made categories like green light, yellow light and, red light for her spending, assigning herself points for each 'green' choice. When she hit a savings goal, she printed it out and posted it on the fridge like a badge of honor.

Suddenly, saving became less about what she was giving up, and more about what she was winning. It was a new kind of scoreboard. A quiet kind of fun.

Your brain is wired for feedback and progress, and it loves small victories. By turning saving into something playful, even competitive, you tap into the same systems that keep people coming back to games and apps. It gives your brain what it craves: visible progress, momentum, and the thrill of the win. But this time, the prize is real.

That's the trick. Saving works better when it feels like something you *get* to do, not something you *should* do. And when you bring in play, with clear rules, achievable goals, and celebrated little wins, you make it feel alive again. It becomes less about restriction, and more about strategy. Not every game needs a leaderboard. But a well-placed challenge? That can flip a habit entirely."

Name Your Future

Labels shape behavior. "Savings Account" sounds abstract like a number you're supposed to care about. But call it your "Escape Fund," "Sabbatical Pot," or "Freedom Account," and it becomes something else entirely: a future you can picture.

That's what happened to Marcus. For years, he transferred money each month, but it felt disconnected, like an obligation. Then one night, almost as a joke, he renamed the account in his banking app: The Mountain Fund. It was a reference to a hiking trip he'd always wanted to take.

Nothing else changed, but something clicked.

He started checking the balance more often. He added little bits here and there. The fund wasn't just money anymore. It was motion toward something real. Motivation didn't have to be forced it just came with the name.

Sometimes, the difference between a habit that sticks and one that fades is just what you call it.

Start Tiny, Grow Steady.

Big ambitions are good. But when it comes to saving, starting too big can backfire. One common mistake is setting an aggressive goal only to burn out or backtrack a few weeks later.

A better approach? Begin with an amount so small it feels almost silly something you won't even notice. Then raise it slowly. Five dollars a week can become fifty by letting each step in between feel normal before you take the next.

The goal is to make saving feel easy, visible, and meaningful. And most importantly, make it feel good. That's when saving sticks and grows.

TRY THIS:

Rename one of your savings accounts today to something that excites you. If you're saving for a trip, for example, call it "Paris Adventure Fund" or "Beach Getaway Fund."

AUTOMATE YOUR SAVINGS: THE SET-AND-FORGET METHOD

Back in Chapter 1, we saw Lisa Carter at her kitchen table, surrounded by bills and bank statements, asking herself two hard questions to reset how she made financial decisions:

Is this moving me closer to the life I want for my family?

Does this bring me peace, or just temporary comfort?

That moment wasn't just reflective it was catalytic. It forced her to confront the reality that most of her spending wasn't grounded in purpose. But as the weeks went by, Lisa also realized something else: clarity alone wasn't enough. She still had to navigate the same daily stress, the same tight margins, the same unexpected expenses. No matter how strong her intention, her system hadn't changed. And without a system, even good intentions eventually give way to exhaustion.

That's when she discovered a better approach one that didn't depend on perfect discipline or daily decisions. It was a simple idea with powerful results: automate the saving process entirely. No tracking. No guilt. No "maybe next month."

At first, it felt like nothing. But a few months later, she checked her balance and saw over a hundred dollars sitting there. It surprised her that she hadn't done anything except not touch it, not notice it, and yet there it was. Hers.

It was the first time saving hadn't felt like a battle. Encouraged, she bumped it up to $20 a week. A year later, she had over $1,000 in her first real emergency fund.

More importantly, she wasn't relying on willpower anymore. The process ran in the background quietly, no longer competing for her attention or energy.

That's the power of the set-and-forget method: it works because it removes friction.

When saving is automatic, it stops being a choice you have to make repeatedly. It becomes a quiet default one that builds wealth in the background while you focus on living your life. You can do the same. Here's how to build a savings system that works without you having to think about it:

1. **Pay Yourself First**
    Set up an automatic transfer from your main account to a savings account every payday. Even a small amount like $10 or $25 can begin to build momentum. The important thing is that it happens before you have a chance to spend.

2. **Use Round-Up Apps**
    Some apps automatically round up your purchases to the nearest dollar and stash the difference. Buy a coffee for $3.50, and it rounds up to $4, saving the extra 50 cents. It sounds small, but over time, those cents turn into serious dollars, effortlessly.

3. **Save the Raise**
    Every time you get a raise or bonus, increase your savings before upgrading your lifestyle. This keeps lifestyle creep in check and allows your savings to grow faster, without feeling like a sacrifice.

TRY THIS:
Set up one automatic transfer today. It doesn't need to be big, just enough to prove to yourself that it's possible. The system will take care of the rest.

THE POWER OF INVISIBLE MONEY – OUT OF SIGHT, OUT OF REACH

Money that's easy to see is easy to spend. When your savings sit in the same account as your daily spending, they don't really feel like savings, they feel available. And availability invites temptation.

That's why one of the simplest ways to save more is to make your money a little harder to reach.

How to Make Your Savings Invisible

Use a separate bank for savings.
When your savings live in a different app, platform, or bank, you create a natural barrier. That extra layer of distance gives you time to pause, and protects you from impulse.

Open a high-yield savings account (HYSA).
Most of these don't offer instant transfers. That small delay, just 24 hours, maybe, can be enough to stop a late-night decision from becoming a withdrawal.

Use lock-in tools for long-term goals.
For things like vacations, large purchases, or a future home, consider fixed deposits, certificates, or time-based investment accounts. When you know the money isn't instantly available, you make plans instead of pulling from it.

These small obstacles may seem inconvenient. But that's the point. A little friction can be the difference between money that grows and money that disappears.

TRY THIS:
Open a separate savings account and transfer a small amount into it today, even $5 is enough to start creating distance.

HOW TO SAVE WITHOUT FEELING DEPRIVED

One of the biggest reasons people avoid saving is the fear that it means cutting out everything they enjoy. But saving doesn't have to feel like sacrifice. In fact, the most effective savers aren't the ones who live on the tightest budgets they're the ones who've learned how to cut waste without cutting joy.

Effortless saving isn't about doing without. It involves noticing what doesn't matter, trimming what you don't miss, and protecting what you truly care about. It's about designing small, smart choices that free up more than you thought possible. The following three strategies show how you can save more without feeling like you're giving something up.

Cut Waste, Not Joy

The fastest way to feel poor is to strip out everything you enjoy in the name of discipline. But smart saving doesn't start with cutting your favorite coffee or skipping the occasional night out. It starts by removing the things you don't even notice. Go through your expenses and look for hidden leaks: old subscriptions, duplicate services, and purchases that don't bring real satisfaction. Redirect those savings toward what actually matters. Protect the things that genuinely bring you joy.

TRY THIS:
Before cutting any expense, ask: "Would I even miss this?" If the answer's no, let it go.

Use Windfalls Wisely

One of the easiest ways to build savings without changing your lifestyle is to harness unexpected money. A birthday gift, a tax refund, a bonus at work, these windfalls don't feel like part of your normal income, which makes them ideal for saving.

The trick is to act fast. Decide ahead of time that any surprise income goes straight to savings, before your brain starts imagining how to spend it.

TRY THIS:

Commit now to saving at least 50% of your next windfall. Send it to a separate account before it blends into your everyday money.

Swap Expensive Habits for Free Joy

You don't need to spend money to enjoy life. Some of the most meaningful experiences – long walks, deep conversations, shared meals, creative play – all cost nothing. The key is to replace, not just remove. If you stop dining out, create a new tradition at home. If you're tempted to shop for comfort, reach for something on your joy list instead.

TRY THIS:

Make a short list of free or low-cost joys that lift you. Keep it visible for the moments when spending becomes your reflex.

FINAL CHALLENGE: THE 30-DAY EFFORTLESS SAVING PLAN

If you've ever struggled to build a savings habit, here's your opportunity to flip the script. This isn't about radical cutbacks or tracking every dollar. It's about proving to yourself that saving can feel simple, doable, even satisfying.

Over the next 30 days, your mission is to install three tiny habits that work together to create real financial momentum:

- **Automate It:**
  Set up an automatic transfer to your savings account, even if it's just a few dollars per week. The point isn't the amount it's the system. Let your money move before you even think about spending it.

- **Rename It:**
  Give your savings account a name that feels personal and exciting. "Emergency Fund" might be practical, but "Freedom Fund" or "Bali 2026" makes the goal feel alive. When you name it, you claim it.

- **No-Spend Days:**
  Once a week, pick a day where you intentionally spend nothing on non-essentials. No quick snacks, no impulse buys. Instead, notice what you reach for out of habit, and transfer the amount you would've spent into savings.

CLOSING THOUGHTS: SAVING IS ABOUT FREEDOM

At its core, saving is about reclaiming choice. It's what builds your freedom in the background, giving you room to breathe, room to move, and room to say yes when it matters most. It's peace of mind in uncertain times. It's the ability to walk away from what no longer serves you. It's knowing, deep down, that you have your own back.

Saving gives you power not just someday, but starting now.

What's Next?

In Chapter 4, we'll explore the surprising connection between clutter and wealth, and how simplifying your life can strengthen your finances. You'll discover how decluttering your space, your schedule, and even your financial habits can create more clarity, control, and room for what truly matters.

Less Stuff, More Freedom: The Link Between Clutter and Wealth

HOW CLUTTER AFFECTS YOUR FINANCES

Tina lived in a cozy two-bedroom apartment in Queens, just far enough from the city to feel a little space, but not quite enough to escape the daily rhythm of New York life. She worked as a project assistant at a design agency and freelanced on weekends, juggling responsibilities like most people she knew: work, bills, errands, life. Tina didn't see herself as someone with a clutter problem. She just liked having options. A few extra jackets for different occasions, backup skincare products when something went on sale, and kitchen tools she might use someday.

Like many of us, she found small ways to reward herself after a long day maybe a candle from that cute store near the office, or a new mug when the old ones started to feel boring. It all felt ordinary, just part of how she lived. But slowly, her space started to feel tighter. Drawers took more effort to close. She found herself buying things she already owned but had forgotten about. Her closet was full, yet she kept defaulting to the same handful of outfits. It wasn't overwhelming, just... tiring.

Then one evening, while getting ready for a friend's dinner party, Tina spent nearly 25 minutes looking for a serving bowl she knew she had somewhere. She never found it, and ended up buying a new one on the way there. It wasn't a big deal, but it made her stop and think. The clutter wasn't chaos, but it was costing her: time. Money. Mental energy. She wasn't drowning in stuff. But the low-level friction was always there, slowing her down, subtly draining her focus, and making everyday decisions harder than they needed to be. Tina realized she didn't need to overhaul her life. She just needed to reset the rhythm, with fewer things to manage and a bit more breathing room.

Her situation isn't unusual. Most of us don't collect things just because of advertising or impulse. Often, it's more personal. Some items make us feel prepared. Others feel tied to who we used to be, or who we're still hoping to become. A drawer of barely used gadgets might reflect plans we haven't acted on yet. A closet of old clothes might hold onto a version of ourselves we're not quite ready to leave behind. In a world that moves fast and encourages constant consumption, it's easy to keep accumulating without noticing the slow cost not just in money, but in mental load. Our homes often reflect more than just our taste. The things that pile up around us can quietly shape how we feel, how we focus, and how we spend.

The connection between our surroundings and our well-being runs deeper than we often realize. This chapter explores how the state of your space affects not just your mood, but your money. A simpler, more intentional environment doesn't just look better it frees up time, lowers stress, and makes it easier to think clearly. And with that clarity, better financial decisions tend to follow. Decluttering isn't about living with nothing. It's about making room mentally, emotionally, and financially for what matters most.

THE TRUE COST OF CLUTTER

The Hidden Financial Costs of Too Much Stuff

Clutter isn't just about mess it's quietly expensive. We often think of our belongings as "already paid for," but the truth is, they continue to cost us long after we bring them home, not always in obvious ways, but in small, persistent leaks of money, focus, and mental bandwidth.

Here are just a few of the ways clutter can quietly strain your finances:

- **Spending on things that don't truly matter**
  Impulse buys often feel harmless in the moment, but they rarely deliver lasting value. Over time, those small comforts can drain resources that could have gone toward something more meaningful.
- **Paying for more space than you need**
  The more you own, the more space you need to store it all, whether that means overflowing closets, off-site storage units, or even a larger home than necessary. And extra space isn't just physical it's financial.
- **Losing value you never recapture**
  Many items like clothes, gadgets, and furniture, start losing value the moment you buy them. When they sit unused, you're not just losing square footage. You're missing out on money you might have reclaimed through reselling or smarter buying choices.
- **Feeding the habit of overconsumption**
  A cluttered space can make it harder to see what you already have. And when you lose track, it becomes easier to keep

accumulating. What starts as convenience slowly turns into a pattern: buy, forget, repeat.

That's exactly what Brian Jacobs came to understand.

On the surface, Brian looked like he had it all together. A top-performing salesman in his mid-thirties, he drove a luxury SUV, carried the latest tech, and had more designer suits than most people would wear in a year. He saw those things as proof that he was winning evidence that he'd made it. But behind the image, he was drowning in credit card debt. His garage was packed with boxes he hadn't opened in years. He paid monthly storage fees to hang onto furniture and electronics he barely remembered owning.

The more he accumulated, the more anxious he became. And the more anxious he felt, the more he spent, trying to preserve the image, to feel in control. What undid him wasn't caused by a single extravagant purchase, but by the steady accumulation of small indulgences each one justified by narratives of success, self-image, and the kind of person he believed he should be.

The turning point?

It came on a quiet Saturday afternoon. Brian was looking for a charger when he opened a drawer he hadn't touched in months, and there it was: a $2,000 watch, still in its box, untouched. He had completely forgotten he even owned it.

But it wasn't just the watch. Beneath it were other expensive things he'd also forgotten: designer belts, limited-edition headphones, a bottle of cologne he'd never opened. Each one had been bought to project a life he thought he wanted.

What unsettled him wasn't the money spent, but the meaning behind it. He saw it clearly now that he'd been curating an image. And all the clutter? It wasn't a collection. It was a trail of choices, proof of how far he'd wandered from what actually mattered.

TRY THIS:

Take a quiet moment and walk through your space. Find five things you spent money on but barely use. Write them down. Add up what they cost. Then ask yourself: Did this bring real value into my life? Would I make the same choice again today?

Sometimes, even a small act of noticing can gently shift how you choose, what you keep, and what you let go of.

DECLUTTERING YOUR SPACE AND YOUR FINANCES

Making Space for What Truly Matters

Making space for what matters is about noticing what no longer adds value and letting it go, piece by piece. The same mindset applies to money: spending with clarity, removing noise, and uncovering what's already working beneath the surface.

If you've ever found something you forgot you owned like a jacket still with the tags, a gift card buried in a drawer, or a tool you replaced twice, you've seen how clutter hides not just things, but resources.

Letting go of the excess reveals more than just space. It can uncover time, ease, and even forgotten money. As the noise fades, what matters starts to come into clearer view. Some people call this minimalism, but at its core, it's just about living with clarity.

The 3-Step Decluttering Process

Now that we've explored the hidden costs of clutter and the surprising rewards of letting go, let's break it down into a simple, actionable process. Decluttering doesn't have to be an all-or-nothing purge. In fact, the most lasting results often come from small, consistent steps, done with intention not urgency. Below is the 3-step decluttering process:

- **Take Stock**
  Start by looking around your home and noticing what's actually useful or meaningful to you. Ask: Do I use this often? Would I miss it if it were gone? This isn't about being strict it's about being honest.
- **Let Go Gently**
  As you move through your things, release what no longer fits the life you're trying to build. Donate, sell, or recycle where it makes sense. You're not erasing the past you're making space for the future.
- **Reset the Space**
  What stays should feel easy to find and easy to keep. Give each item a clear place, so your environment supports you instead of pulling on your attention. When your space feels calm, it becomes easier to think, plan, and live with intention.

TRY THIS:
Pick one small area today a drawer, a shelf, or a corner of your desk and declutter it. Once you've finished, take a moment to pause and notice the difference. That feeling of clarity and lightness? That's momentum

SELLING CLUTTER TO BOOST YOUR SAVINGS

Turning Clutter into Cash

Most people don't realize they're sitting on a hidden financial opportunity right in their own homes. The excess items taking up space in closets, basements, and cabinets aren't just clutter they're untapped savings.

Lisa Carter was one of those people. After automating her savings back in Chapter 3, she began noticing how much stuff she still held onto: things she no longer used, didn't need, or had emotionally outgrown. Motivated by her new mindset, she listed a few items online: an old couch, an extra TV, and some kitchen gadgets collecting dust. In just one month, she earned $1,200. She transferred every dollar into her emergency fund. What surprised her wasn't just the money it was how light she felt afterward. Letting go of the physical clutter made space, emotionally and financially. It reminded her that saving isn't always about cutting back. Sometimes, it's about releasing what no longer serves you.

Here's How You Can Turn Your Clutter Into Cash:
- **Identify items with potential resale value**, such as electronics, designer clothing, collectibles, books, unused furniture, and anything in good condition you no longer use.

- **Use online marketplaces:** Sites like eBay, Vinted, Facebook Marketplace, and Poshmark make it easy to reach buyers near and far. Good photos and honest descriptions go a long way.
- **Create a dedicated 'Declutter Fund':** Funnel all proceeds into a specific goal: your emergency savings, debt payoff, or investment account. Naming the fund makes it more motivating.

TRY THIS:

Pick one item to sell this week and move the proceeds into savings. This simple step will get you started on your decluttering journey and build momentum for future efforts.

THE MINIMALIST SPENDING MINDSET

Changing How You Buy Moving Forward

Decluttering your space is only part of the equation. The deeper shift happens when you change how new things enter your life. True minimalism is about choosing what you don't invite in. Adopting a minimalist spending mindset helps you resist the cycle of accumulation and stay focused on what truly matters. It's a way of living that emphasizes intentionality, not denial.

Figures like Marie Kondo and The Minimalists popularized it through the lens of simplicity and design. Still, at its core, it's about reclaiming control of your money, your space, and your attention. Once you begin to see clutter for what it really costs in time, money, and mental bandwidth, it becomes easier to pause before bringing more in. Minimalist spending creates breathing room: fewer regrets, fewer impulse buys, more clarity.

1. Before you make a new purchase, ask yourself:
2. Do I really need this, or is it an impulse?
3. Give yourself a cooling-off window. A 24-hour pause often turns a "must-have" into a "no thanks."
4. Will this add long-term value?
5. Does it enhance your routine, bring genuine joy, or serve a clear purpose aligned with your goals?
6. Could this money be better used elsewhere?
7. Could it fuel your emergency fund, chip away at debt, or go toward a future experience that matters more?

These questions aren't meant to restrict you, but to protect your focus. Each purchase is a decision not just about money, but about the kind of life you're building.

TRY THIS:
For your next non-essential purchase, wait 24 hours before buying. That pause might be the space you need to make a better decision.

FINAL CHALLENGE: THE 7-DAY DECLUTTERING EXPERIMENT

Experience What It Feels Like to Breathe Easier Mentally and Financially

Here's your 7-day experiment:

1. **Declutter One Small Area Each Day**
   Start simple: a drawer, a shelf, a corner of your closet. One small win each day builds powerful momentum.

2. **Sell or Donate at Least One Item Per Day**
   Each day, choose one item to release. Whether you sell it or give it away, you're freeing space, and possibly gaining cash to boost your savings goals.

3. **Track the Money Saved from Avoiding Unnecessary Purchases**
   This week, pause before impulse purchases. At the end of each day, note what you *didn't* buy, and how much you saved. You might be surprised by what that awareness reveals

Your Goal: To experience, firsthand, how owning less can feel like more. By the end of seven days, your space will be lighter, your finances clearer, and your mind freer. Not from perfection, but from progress you can feel.

CLOSING THOUGHTS: FREEDOM COMES FROM OWNING LESS

In a culture that often equates success with accumulation, it's easy to forget that every item we own costs us something not just money, but time, attention, and energy. True wealth is found in clarity, freedom, and intentional living, rather than endless acquiring.

When you own only what supports the life you want, you reclaim more than just space you reclaim power. Power to say no to distractions. Power to direct your resources toward your goals. And most importantly, the power to live in alignment with your values. Letting go of the excess means making room for more of the right kind of joy the kind that's sustainable, intentional, and deeply your own.

YOUR NEXT STEP:

Pick one decluttering habit and put it into action today. Whether it's clearing a single drawer, selling something you no longer use, or pausing before your next purchase, that one simple step can create real momentum. Freedom doesn't begin with a massive overhaul; it begins with a single, intentional move.

What's Next?

In Chapter 5, we'll shift gears from simplifying your space to expanding your income. You'll learn how to unlock new earning opportunities without sacrificing the financial clarity and peace you've started building.

Know Your Worth: Unlocking Your Earning Potential

THE LOYALTY TRAP

Erica Lewis had always prided herself on being dependable. For five years, she was the quiet engine of a mid-sized marketing firm in Denver. She showed up early, stayed late, and took on extra projects without being asked. She trained new hires, ran point on campaigns, and kept things moving when no one else stepped up.

Promotions never came, but praise did. People said things like, "We don't know what we'd do without you," and "You're the glue of this team." Erica believed them. So she stayed loyal, kept her head down, and trusted that her hard work would eventually be rewarded.

Then came Natalie. She was sharp, confident, and quick to learn. Erica found herself training her through the same systems she had once learned alone. Over lunch one afternoon, Natalie casually mentioned her starting salary. Erica nearly dropped her fork. Natalie was earning twelve thousand dollars more. They held the same title, shared the same responsibilities, and worked in the same office.

Later that evening, Erica sat at her kitchen table, laptop open, heart heavy. She searched salary data, reread her original offer letter, and replayed the lunch conversation over and over in her mind. What unsettled her most wasn't Natalie's confidence. It was the realization that the system had overlooked her, that it chose to reward boldness over loyalty, and negotiation over quiet contribution. The same system that praised her dedication had underpaid her for years, simply because she never asked for more.

Believing that hard work would be enough didn't make her naïve. It made her human. Many people carry that hope, trusting that patience and dedication will eventually be recognized. Often, it isn't.

While Erica had waited to be recognized, Natalie had negotiated from the start and received it. She hadn't worked harder or longer. She had simply entered from the outside, where the rules were different. But for Erica, the lesson was already clear. She wasn't underpaid because she lacked skill or value. She was underpaid because the system counted on her not questioning it. That night was a turning point.

Why You're Probably Undervaluing Yourself

Most people treat their first salary offer like a fixed truth as if that number reflects their worth, rather than what someone else hopes they'll accept. But that number is rarely based on your full potential. It's shaped by what you're willing to ask for, what the company thinks it can get away with, and how clearly you understand the value you bring.

Your earning potential isn't fixed nor is it defined by your degree, your job title, or how grateful you feel to be hired.

It's a muscle one that grows stronger every time you build rare skills, speak your value out loud, and stop confusing loyalty with compensation.

Consider this:

- Many people are underpaid because they never ask for more not because they lack talent.
- Most employees skip negotiation entirely, either out of discomfort, fear, or the assumption that *"they'll notice me eventually."*
- Over time, this leads to silent financial stagnation leaving tens of thousands of dollars behind simply because they didn't challenge the first offer.

This chapter is about reclaiming that power. You'll learn how to move beyond passive acceptance and start earning with intention whether that means negotiating a raise, pivoting to higher-paying roles, or building side income streams aligned with your strengths.

This is your roadmap to unlocking your income ceiling and building wealth not just by saving more, but by earning more, confidently and consciously.

IDENTIFYING YOUR TRUE MARKET VALUE

Step 1: Research What You're Worth

Most people underestimate their worth not because they lack ability, but because they lack information. They rely on gut feelings, outdated assumptions, or their employer's silence, rather than doing the real work of understanding their market value. But if you don't know what your skills are worth, you can't confidently ask for or walk toward what you truly deserve. Determining your value in the marketplace takes intentional effort. Here's how to get clear:

Check industry benchmarks: Use platforms like Glassdoor, LinkedIn Salary, Payscale, and Salarytransparentstreet.com. These sites aggregate real-world compensation data by job title, experience level, location, and industry.

1. **Talk to real people in your field:** If you have mentors or trusted peers, ask them (respectfully) about typical pay ranges. Even vague numbers like "above six figures" or "around 80K" help sharpen your sense of reality.

2. **Study relevant job postings**: Search for roles that match your experience and skills. Pay attention to the salary bands when listed, or use the role requirements to gauge where you stand.

Employers don't always pay based on loyalty or tenure. They pay based on what people request, and what they're prepared to walk away from.

TRY THIS:

Block out one focused hour this week. Research your job title, skills, and industry. Use at least two online salary tools. Compare the results to your current income.

Step 2: Assess Your Unique Value Proposition

Your market value isn't just based on your job title or how many years you've been working. It's based on the value you *actually* create and how clearly you understand and communicate that value. Most people don't realize how much they truly contribute.

They show up, do great work, and assume someone will notice. But recognition is rarely automatic. You have to know your worth and speak it.

To uncover your true value, ask yourself:

- **What do I do exceptionally well?** Are there skills, certifications, or areas of expertise that set you apart in your role or industry?
- **What results have I produced?** Think in terms of impact: revenue generated, costs reduced, clients gained, projects delivered, teams led. Numbers speak.
- **What perspective do I bring?** Your background, lived experiences, or unique approach to problem-solving may offer real value that others can't replicate.

Lisa Carter once believed that being dependable and hardworking would eventually speak for itself. But when she finally sat down to document her contributions the new clients she brought in, the money she helped save, the extra roles she took on it was like seeing her career through a new lens. She realized she wasn't just filling a role; she was driving results. She was an asset. That shift in perception gave her the clarity and confidence to ask for a raise, and this time, she didn't downplay her worth. She got the raise and more importantly, she finally believed she had earned it.

TRY THIS:

Create a one-page "impact resume" for yourself. Not the kind you'd submit in a job application, but a list of real contributions you've made, measurable outcomes, leadership moments, and examples of above-and-beyond work. Read it out loud to yourself. You may be surprised by how much power you've been under-crediting.

Step 3: Factor in Location and Industry Trends

Knowing your worth means understanding not just your skills, but also where those skills are most valued. Your salary isn't determined in a vacuum. It's shaped by your geographic location, industry, and current demand for your role. Take this example: A data analyst in San Francisco might earn $110,000, while someone with the same skills and experience in Nashville might earn $80,000. It's not that the San Francisco analyst is more talented; it's that the cost of living is higher, companies are competing for talent, and tech-driven roles tend to command higher pay in that region.

Industries work the same way. A project manager in healthcare or tech may see higher pay than a project manager in education or the nonprofit sector, even if they work just as hard. Staying informed about location and industry trends helps you negotiate more effectively, make better job decisions, and even plan relocations or upskilling strategically.

Ask yourself:

- What's the average salary for my role in different cities?
- Are wages rising in my industry or staying flat?
- Are my skills part of a growing trend (e.g., AI, remote ops, green energy)?

TRY THIS:
Search for your job title on platforms like Glassdoor or Levels.fyi and compare compensation across cities. Look at at least three locations, including where you live now. You might discover that you're being underpaid, or that you could command more elsewhere, remotely or in person.

HOW TO NEGOTIATE A RAISE (AND ACTUALLY GET IT)

Negotiation is one of the fastest, most underused ways to increase your income. Yet many people avoid it, not because they don't need the money, but because they're afraid of hearing "no," or they've never been taught how to ask.

Here's the truth: most companies expect employees to negotiate. In fact, many initial offers or current salaries leave room for adjustment. Failing to negotiate doesn't just cost you once; it compounds over time, leaving tens of thousands (even hundreds of thousands) of dollars on the table throughout your career. Let's fix that.

The 3-Step Raise Formula:

Prove Your Value
Before you ever schedule a meeting, gather evidence. Create a short list of your specific contributions:

1. Did you save the company money?
2. Bring in new clients?

3. Solve a major problem?

4. Train or lead others?

The key is to quantify your impact wherever possible. Numbers speak. So do outcomes. If you've gone above and beyond your role, make that visible.

Know Your Number

Once you've done the research (see previous section), set a realistic but confident salary target. Don't just pull a number from the air. Anchor it in:

- Market benchmarks for your role and city
- Your experience and responsibilities
- Industry trends and company health

And don't forget: compensation isn't only about base salary. Consider negotiating:

- Extra vacation time
- Remote work flexibility
- A learning and development budget
- Health or retirement benefits

These can often be easier to secure and just as valuable.

Make the Ask

Schedule a focused, professional meeting with your manager. Don't drop this in passing. Treat it like the business case it is. When you sit down, lead with clarity and calm confidence:

"Over the past year, I've taken on [list responsibilities]. I've also contributed to [list impact or metrics]. Based on my market research and the value I've delivered, I believe a salary adjustment to [$X] is appropriate."

Then pause. Let the silence work for you. Expect some discussion. That's normal. But unless you're given a firm and justified no, stay grounded in your value. Most raises are won not with aggression, but with preparation and composure.

Claiming Her Worth: How Erica Turned Clarity into Confidence

Erica had never negotiated before. But hearing others' success stories gave her the courage to try. She prepared a one-page summary of her accomplishments, highlighting the new hires she had trained, the cross-team project she led, and the client account she helped retain.

She was nervous at first, but she pushed forward and prepared meticulously. She practiced her ask and scheduled the meeting. When the moment came, she delivered her pitch confidently, just as she had rehearsed.

The result? She didn't just walk away with a $10,000 raise; she also secured an extra week of paid vacation, a flexible remote-work arrangement, and a professional development stipend she could use for courses she had long postponed.

It wasn't just about the money. It was about what the money and the extras represented: that she was no longer waiting quietly to be noticed. She was finally claiming the value she had always brought to the table.

TRY THIS:
Write down three clear reasons why you deserve a raise. Practice your pitch with a trusted friend or mentor. Then, schedule the conversation. The discomfort of asking is temporary, but the upside could last for years.

A Note on Reality:

Not every story ends like Erica's, and that's important to acknowledge. You can prepare well, make a strong case, and still hear no. When that happens, it's not a reflection of your value; it's often a reflection of how your current workplace values you. If a company consistently underappreciates your contributions, despite clear evidence and respectful requests, it may be a sign to seek an environment where your skills are recognized, rewarded, and respected. Negotiation isn't just about securing more money; it's about discovering your worth and refusing to settle for less than what you deserve.

OVERCOMING COMMON NEGOTIATION FEARS

It's natural to feel nervous about asking for more. Many people stay underpaid for years, not because they lack talent, but because they let fear lead the conversation. But fear, left unchallenged, quietly chips away at your potential. Let's name the most common ones, and dismantle them:

- **Fear of Rejection:**
  "What if they say no?"
  Reframe it: What if they say yes? The worst-case scenario is rarely as bad as it seems. A respectful ask backed by evidence

rarely burns bridges. But silence guarantees nothing changes. Every raise that's ever been given started with someone willing to ask.

- **Fear of Being Seen as Greedy:**
You're not greedy for wanting to be fairly compensated. You're professional. Companies expect negotiation, it's not a sign of entitlement, it's a signal of awareness. Asking for what you've earned isn't arrogance. It's self-respect.

- **Fear of Losing Your Job:**
Let's be honest: if asking for a raise puts your job at risk that says more about the employer than about you. Great companies value open conversations and want their talent to feel supported. A raise conversation, done thoughtfully, actually shows maturity and long-term commitment.

TRY THIS:

Write down your top two fears around negotiating a raise. Then challenge each one with facts:

- What evidence do you have that the fear is true?
- What evidence do you have that it isn't?
- What would you say to a friend who had the same fear?

Now, reframe each fear into a possibility:

Instead of "What if they say no?" → try "What if they say yes?"

Instead of "I might seem greedy," → try "I'm setting a professional standard."

This small exercise turns vague anxiety into clear thinking, and helps you move from hesitation to action.

CREATING NEW INCOME STREAMS

Your employer is not your only source of wealth.

For most people, a paycheck is the primary, sometimes only, income stream. But in today's economy, that model is no longer sufficient. Relying solely on your employer for financial growth is like standing on one leg: any instability can throw you off balance.

James Reynolds learned this the hard way.

After building a strong case for a raise, his manager told him the budget was too tight. No promotion. No pay bump. Just a pat on the back and "maybe next quarter." At first, James felt discouraged. But then he realized something empowering:

He couldn't control the company's budget, but he could control his initiative. He had always been good at graphic design, so he started offering freelance services to small businesses through Upwork and Fiverr. Within six months, he was making an extra $1,500 a month, on his terms. His takeaway: Your income ceiling at work doesn't have to be the ceiling for your entire life.

Ways to Make More Money Outside Your Job

Whether you're looking to cover more expenses, accelerate your savings goals, or simply reduce your financial dependence on one paycheck, here are proven ways to earn more:

- **Freelancing**
  Sell your skills directly to the global market. Sites like Upwork, Fiverr, and Toptal allow you to offer services in writing, design, coding, marketing, editing, and more. Freelancing allows you

to manage your schedule, set your rates, and decide which clients you want to work with.

- **Side Hustles**

  A side hustle is any way of earning money that you take on in addition to your primary job. Consider options like coaching, tutoring, consulting, hosting workshops, or creating digital products such as templates, courses, or eBooks. Pick something that aligns with your skills and interests it'll be much easier to stay consistent.

- **Passive income**

  Passive income means creating a system or asset once that keeps producing value over time with minimal ongoing effort. Maybe you've considered launching an online course, starting a blog that brings in ad revenue, or investing in dividend-paying stocks. These ventures often require significant upfront effort, but once established, they can earn money in the background, helping you break free from the constant cycle of trading time for income.

TRY THIS:

Think of one way you could start earning extra income with the skills you already possess. Is there something friends or colleagues consistently ask you for help with? It might be design tips, writing feedback, tech troubleshooting, photography, or even organizing spaces. Pick one area to focus on and take a small, tangible step today. That could be creating a simple online profile, letting a friend know you're available for work, or jotting down an idea you've been meaning to explore.

Developing High-Income Skills

Every skill has value, but a few have the power to significantly boost your earning potential, unlocking access to better-paying jobs, freelance gigs, or unexpected business opportunities.

Marcus understood this when he realized his salary had hit a ceiling. Another degree wouldn't break the ceiling; he needed leverage. After some research, he stumbled upon copywriting. It felt approachable, and more importantly, it aligned with how he thought and communicated. He committed to learning it, reading, practicing, and watching tutorials on nights and weekends. Three months later, he closed his first deal, a modest campaign that paid him $300 for a weekend's work. It wasn't life-changing money, but it was proof. What started as curiosity was now undeniably a viable income stream.

In today's world, high-income skills often fall into three broad categories. The first is technical ability: coding, data analysis, cybersecurity, even AI prompt engineering or cloud architecture. These are the engines behind the digital economy. The second is persuasion: sales, negotiation, communication, because in nearly every industry, the ability to clearly present ideas and move others to action is rare and highly rewarded. The third is creative business literacy: marketing, copywriting, branding, digital advertising, and content creation. These are the skills that help ideas spread and companies grow.

Just one, done well, can raise your value dramatically, whether you use it inside your job or out in the world on your terms.

TRY THIS:

Think about a skill you've always been curious about, maybe something you've seen others use to earn more or create new opportunities. Watch a tutorial, download a free guide, or spend just 30 focused minutes exploring it.

FINAL CHALLENGE: THE 30-DAY INCOME BOOST PLAN

For the next 30 days, commit to taking clear, actionable steps to boost your income. Here's how you can start:

1. **Research your industry's pay:** Set aside time to explore the average salary for your role in your region. Use trusted sources like Glassdoor, Payscale, or industry-specific reports to see where you stand, and define a target salary that reflects your skills and experience.

2. **Take action toward negotiating a raise:** If you're employed, gather evidence of your results and contributions, then prepare to request a raise, ideally during a review or scheduled check-in. If you're self-employed, reassess your pricing and consider increasing your rates for new or premium clients.

3. **Explore one new income stream:** Choose a potential new way to earn, like freelancing, launching a side hustle, or starting to invest, and take the first actionable step. That might mean signing up on a freelance platform, outlining a business idea, or opening an investment account.

Your Goal: By the end of these 30 days, you should have a stronger grasp of your market value, a clear strategy for negotiating higher pay, and one new income stream actively in progress.

CLOSING THOUGHTS: YOU CONTROL YOUR EARNING POTENTIAL

Think of your income as flexible, a lever you can learn to pull, regardless of where it comes from, whether from an employer, clients, or digital platforms. Your income is something you can actively influence and grow by developing high-value skills, negotiating strategically, and building multiple income streams to take charge of your financial future. This chapter was about earning more by reclaiming your agency in a system that often conditions you to settle.

YOUR NEXT STEP:

Choose one action and take it today: research your market value, draft your raise pitch, or launch that freelance profile, because momentum begins with a single move, and you'll be surprised how quickly things shift once you do.

What's Next?

In Chapter 6, we'll move from earning to spending, diving into the hidden psychological traps that influence our financial behavior. Why do we buy things we don't need? Why is saving so difficult? And how can we retrain our minds to build lasting, meaningful wealth?

The Hidden Forces Behind Your Spending Habits

WHY WE SPEND MORE THAN WE SHOULD

Have you ever caught yourself in a store, holding an item you never intended to buy, wondering how it ended up in your hands? Or maybe you were halfway through a late-night scroll and clicked "Buy Now" without really thinking, only to realize, once the confirmation email arrived, that you never made a conscious decision to buy it.

It's easy to shrug it off. Returns are simple, the charge is temporary, and the receipts' already in your inbox. You'll deal with it later. But the truth is, most of us never do. And even when we follow through and send something back, we're still left with the feeling that we slipped, that moment of impulse, the mental clutter that comes from undoing what didn't need to happen in the first place.

Overspending isn't really about being careless or bad with money, even though that's how we usually frame it or brush it off. Most of the time, it's just what happens when you're moving through a world that's been quietly designed to work around your better judgment. It's not just about willpower or the odd temptation here and there. The systems consisting of apps, ads, shops, and websites are built to tap into the weak spots in how our minds work.

It doesn't always feel like pressure, but it's there. These little things quietly steer us toward spending, whether it's the fear of missing out, a flash sale banner that says "just dropped" when you weren't even looking, or those little messages telling us there are only two items left in stock. Most of the time, we don't stop to question it. We keep moving through spaces such as stores, apps, and websites that are set up to guide us to the checkout without much resistance. Autoplay videos, endless scroll, and one-click buttons, keep us engaged just long enough for a purchase to slip through.

And then there's social media, which cranks up the pressure. Algorithms keep us swimming in comparison, until something we barely noticed a minute ago suddenly feels essential. Notifications add urgency we didn't ask for. Even something as simple as a "like" can shift our thinking, making us equate being seen or admired with owning the thing we saw.

This kind of advertising goes beyond just catching your attention. It's built to influence behavior, scaled up and embedded into the way we live now. You see it in the apps you open without thinking, the ads you scroll past but still absorb, the suggestions that seem to know what you want before you do. It lowers the effort. It makes spending feel like the natural next step, something you do almost without choosing.

The result? A cycle of impulse buying, lifestyle creep, and financial anxiety. A loop that can be hard to step out of.

This chapter will help you understand the psychology behind your spending, recognize the emotional and social triggers that influence your habits, and give you practical tools to bring your financial choices back in line with what actually matters to you.

THE PSYCHOLOGY OF SPENDING – HOW STORES INFLUENCE YOU WITHOUT YOU NOTICING

Why You Spend When You Didn't Plan To

Have you ever found yourself adding something to your cart you hadn't planned to buy just because it was "on sale," or there was a timer ticking down? You're not alone. These aren't random impulses; they're often the result of deliberate design.

Retailers and marketers spend billions studying consumer behavior. Their goal? To make spending feel irresistible, using subtle psychological nudges that bypass logic and speak directly to emotion.

Let's explore some of the most common techniques, and how to spot them before they cost you.

1. **Limited-Time Offers: Manufactured Urgency**
   "Sale ends tonight!" or "Only 3 left at this price!" These phrases are crafted to trigger FOMO (Fear of Missing Out). Timers, scarcity labels, and urgent messaging hijack your decision-making system, rushing you past careful thought and straight into "Buy Now."
   It's not that you needed the item; it's that you feared regretting not acting.

2. **Charm Pricing: The 99-Cent Illusion**
   Why is $9.99 so common? Because your brain processes that
   first digit more heavily than the rest. This "left-digit bias"
   makes $9.99 feel cheaper than $10, even though the difference
   is just one cent. That tiny tweak drives billions in revenue.

3. **Subscription Traps: Auto-Renew and Forget**
   Many services from media streaming to razors to meal kits
   hook you with a low intro rate, then silently auto-renew. Over
   time, you may keep paying long after you've stopped using the
   service. These "invisible drains" can quietly bleed your budget.
   Quick fix: Review your subscriptions monthly. Cancel
   anything you haven't used in the past 30 days.

4. **Buy More, Save More: The Overspend Trap**
   "Get 3 for the price of 2!" sounds like a bargain, until you
   realize you only needed one. Bulk discounts encourage
   overbuying, often for things you won't use anytime soon. That
   extra bottle of shampoo? It's not saving you money if it ends
   up collecting dust.

5. **Decoy Pricing: The Illusion of Value**
   You see three coffee sizes: Small $2.00, Medium $3.00, Large
   $4.50. The large feels like a "better deal", even if it's more than
   you need. That's a pricing strategy designed to steer you
   toward higher spending without you noticing.

Real Life: Chris's Wake-Up Call

Chris never thought of himself as someone who had a spending
problem. He didn't buy expensive watches or fly first class. But over
time, his purchases started adding up in ways he hadn't really
noticed. Instagram was usually the trigger he'd be lying on the

couch, scrolling through his feed, and suddenly there'd be something that made his life feel smaller. Someone on a trip. Someone showing off a new pair of shoes. Someone posting their "essentials."

So he'd buy something, usually nothing huge. Just enough to feel like he wasn't falling behind. A new hoodie. Some sneakers he'd seen in an ad. Another thing he didn't really need, but it made him feel a little more in control, like he was still in the game.

One morning, he checked his bank account and froze. The number wasn't shocking, but the pattern was. None of the purchases were worth regretting on their own, but stacked together, they told a story he hadn't meant to write a story where he'd been drifting, spending without really noticing.

It was the sudden awareness that all that spending had been for people who weren't even thinking about him. People who'd never notice if he didn't post the shoes. Or the trip. Or anything at all.

TRY THIS:

Before your next non-essential purchase, pause for 10 seconds. Ask yourself: "Was I looking for this item or did something push me toward it?" That moment of clarity can break the chain reaction, and put your choices back in your control.

EMOTIONAL SPENDING – BUYING HAPPINESS (THAT DOESN'T LAST)

We don't just spend because we need things; we spend because we feel things. Emotional spending is one of the most common and most quietly destructive drivers of financial stress. It often begins in moments of discomfort: stress after a hard day, boredom on a quiet evening, sadness after an argument. In those moments, buying something new feels like a relief, a way to boost your mood, or a temporary escape. And for a little while, it is.

Clicking the "Add to Cart", the tap on "Buy Now", gives your brain a hit of dopamine. It feels good, giving you a brief emotional high. But like all quick fixes, the effect fades fast. What's left behind is often regret, clutter, or debt, and none of the emotional healing you were hoping to buy.

Decision Fatigue Makes It Worse

You make hundreds of small choices every day: what to wear, what to answer, what to ignore, what to cook, what to put off. By the time evening rolls around, you're running low on energy, even if you didn't do anything "big." This is what psychologists call decision fatigue. And when your brain is tired, it's more likely to take the path of least resistance reaching for your phone, opening your favorite shopping app, and telling yourself you deserve something small. The more drained you feel, the more tempting that little reward becomes.

The Deeper Pattern

This is just something your brain learns. Spending brings a brief sense of relief, so your mind starts to associate it with feeling better. You feel low, you make a purchase, you get a small lift... then it's gone. But the cycle is familiar, and that familiarity starts to feel like comfort. Over time, it turns into a pattern: you don't shop for the item, you shop for the feeling. But no item can do the work of healing what's underneath.

Every time you try to buy your way out of discomfort, the gap between what you're feeling and what you truly need just gets a little wider.

Trigger States: The Invisible Starting Point

Most emotionally driven spending can be traced back to a few recurring emotional states. They act like invisible pressure points, subtle, powerful, and easy to overlook:

- Stress: you've had a long day, your brain is overloaded, and spending becomes a way to reclaim a sense of ease or reward.
- Boredom: you're not really looking for anything; you're just looking for something. Shopping becomes stimulation, and a form of escape.
- Loneliness or Sadness: the thing you're buying isn't the point. It's the idea of feeling comfort or connection.
- Celebration: you're feeling good, and somewhere along the way, spending became the automatic way to mark the moment.

These are predictable psychological states that marketing teams know well and advertisers, apps, and algorithms quietly build around. And that's not something to feel ashamed about. It's something to notice. Because once you can see what's happening, once you name the state you're in, you create space for a different kind of choice.

How to Stop Emotional Spending:

Most people don't even realize they're spending emotionally until the habit's already formed. Maybe it happens after a long day, or when things feel flat, or when something hurts and you don't know what else to do. Emotional cues have a way of slipping under the radar, but they shape how we spend more than we think.

That's why keeping a short-term spending journal can be so revealing. It helps you spot recurring situations and emotional states that lead you to spend. Write down what you bought and how you felt before you bought it. Over time, patterns start to show up. You realize you weren't buying things because you needed them; you were buying because you were trying to feel better.

Once you've identified your patterns, create a simple pause. One of the easiest ways to do this is with the 24-hour rule. If it's not essential, don't buy it right away. Wait a day. Just that small delay can take the edge off the urgency. Something that felt like a must-have in the moment often fades when given space. You'll be giving yourself space to choose with clarity instead of compulsion.

Equally important is building healthier emotional habits. If you shop when you're stressed, bored, or low, redirect the impulse. Read a few pages of a good book. Go for a walk. Listen to music. Celebrate a win with a phone call to a friend, not a checkout screen. These shifts don't just help you avoid unnecessary spending; they help you replace it with something more emotionally nourishing.

That doesn't mean cutting out joy or spontaneity. It simply means budgeting for it. Set aside a small, intentional amount each month for guilt-free enjoyment. When that treat is planned, it no longer carries the emotional weight of a hidden trigger; it becomes a reward you've anticipated and chosen with intention.

Ava's Turning Point?

Ava started asking herself one quiet question before she bought anything:

"Am I buying this because I need it or because I'm trying to change how I feel?"

That single habit saved her hundreds of dollars over a few months. But more than that, it helped her break the emotional loop. Spending was no longer a reflex. It became a choice.

> **TRY THIS:**
> For one week, track your impulse purchases. Next to each, write down how you were feeling at the time. At the end of the week, review the patterns. Which emotions cost you the most? Which ones can you meet differently, without opening your wallet?

THE INFLUENCE OF SOCIAL MEDIA AND LIFESTYLE INFLATION

Not all spending comes from emotional impulse. Sometimes, it comes from comparison that's subtle, constant, and hard to detect. In a world where social media blurs the line between inspiration and expectation, we don't just see how others live; we begin to absorb the idea that this is how we should live too.

Platforms like Instagram and TikTok turn everyday scrolling into a steady drip of luxury, polish, and curated perfection. A vacation photo here, a new apartment there. It doesn't shout, but it suggests that this is what success looks like. And before we realize it, we start measuring our own lives against images crafted by strangers.

The shift is gradual. A jacket we wouldn't have looked at last year now feels essential. A restaurant we used to skip starts to feel like the new normal. A home upgrade moves from a "nice idea" to a "need." It's not just about wanting nicer things; it's about proving something making a statement that shows we're doing okay or that we belong.

This is how lifestyle inflation sets in. As our income grows, our spending grows right along with it, not always because we need more, but because our definition of enough has been quietly reprogrammed. We stretch to match an identity we didn't consciously choose, chasing a life that may have little to do with what truly matters to us.

Chris's Wake-Up Call?

For a while, Chris believed that success had a certain look. A new car meant he was doing well. The right brands in his closet, luxury vacations on his feed it all felt like progress, like he was finally getting somewhere.

But a year in, he looked at his bank account and felt the opposite. The numbers were going in the wrong direction, his debt was growing, and the stress to keep up was constant. None of it was making him feel better. It wasn't the fulfillment he thought he was working toward.

The issue wasn't just overspending; it was how he'd started measuring his life against someone else's version of success. The real cost of comparison is the erosion of self-trust. It chips away at your sense of enough. It makes you second-guess your path. And over time, it turns life into something more expensive than it needs to be in all ways that matter, especially in terms of money and real peace of mind.

How to Resist Social Pressure Spending

Resisting the pull of social media spending begins with reclaiming control over what enters your mental space. One of the most powerful financial decisions you can make doesn't involve money at all, it's deciding who you follow. Curate your digital environment deliberately as if it matters, because it does. If certain accounts leave you feeling behind, restless, or suddenly convinced you need something you didn't care about five minutes ago, it's okay to unfollow. Protecting your peace and your financial path is more valuable than keeping up with a curated feed of other people's highlight reels.

But avoidance alone isn't enough. What helps most is having something real to move toward. So, anchor yourself in financial goals that feel genuinely exciting to you, not just admirable on paper. Maybe it's finally becoming debt-free. Maybe it's saving for time off to do something that fills you back up. Maybe it's just having breathing room every month. Whatever the goal, it must be emotionally resonant enough to compete with the temptation of someone else's lifestyle.

And when comparison shows up again, as it probably will, try to remind yourself that this isn't the whole story. Most of what you're seeing online is edited, filtered, and framed to look effortless. You don't see the bills behind the outfits, the burnout behind the beach photos, or the loneliness that sometimes sits just outside the frame. Comparing your full life to someone else's highlight reel is a game no one wins.

TRY THIS:

Unfollow one account today that makes you feel pressured to spend. Replace it with an account that inspires financial freedom.

The Art of Conscious Spending: Where Money Meets Meaning

True financial mastery is about becoming more intentional in how you create joy with your money. Think of your money as seeds that, when planted with care, grow into experiences, security, and satisfaction that last much longer than any impulse buy.

Start by redefining what "worth it" means to you. That new phone might be tempting, but would the same money bring more meaning through a weekend away with close friends? A concert you'll remember for years? Pottery classes that bring your creativity back to life? Research confirms what many of us already feel: memories outlast possessions. Before you swipe to make that purchase, ask whether this money could create something you'll still care about a year from now.

Even how you spend changes how you feel about it. There's often wisdom in using cash or a debit card, in watching your balance shift in real time, or physically handing over money. These small, tangible moments create natural pauses. You slow down just long enough to ask: Does this still feel like a good idea?

But conscious spending doesn't mean living under a strict financial diet. Just like a good garden needs space for wildflowers, your budget needs space for joy. Set aside a "joy fund", something small to light you up, but deliberate. Maybe it's for fresh flowers on your desk. Maybe it's for that book you've been eyeing. Maybe it's for impromptu pizza with a friend after a long day. When pleasure is planned, it stops being impulsive. It becomes sustainable self-care.

And then comes the quietest, most powerful part: reflection. Each month, or even after each pay cycle, take a moment to look back. Look back to understand. What did your money actually go toward? Which choices felt aligned with your values, and which felt off? Like an archaeologist studying artifacts, you begin to see patterns: a growing savings account, a donation that still makes you smile, or a few purchases that don't quite sit right. This feedback gives you the chance to course-correct with clarity.

Because money is more than numbers, it's the currency of your life story. Spend it consciously, and you'll find yourself richer in ways that have nothing to do with your bank balance, and everything to do with living a life that feels genuinely, deeply yours.

TRY THIS:

Write down your top three financial priorities, then look at your recent purchases. If there's a gap between what you say matters and where your money is going, that's a clue, a signal, and an invitation to realign.

FINAL CHALLENGE: THE 7-DAY NO-SPEND EXPERIMENT

To put everything you've learned into practice, take on this 7-day no-spend challenge:

- **Avoid All Non-Essential Spending:** For one week, commit to spending only on essentials, such as groceries, utilities, and transportation.
- **Write Down Every Temptation:** Whenever the urge to make a non-essential purchase strikes, write it down. Please include the item, its price, and the reason you wanted to buy it.
- **Reflect on What You Truly Missed:** At the end of the week, review your list and reflect on whether you truly missed out on anything. Chances are, you'll realize that most of those purchases weren't necessary.

Your Goal: Use this experiment to uncover how much of your spending is driven by emotions versus actual needs.

CLOSING THOUGHTS: RECLAIM CONTROL OVER YOUR MONEY

True financial well-being begins with awareness. Noticing the quiet patterns behind how and why you spend. When you begin to see the emotional, social, and psychological pulls at work, you start spending in a way that reflects your values, and not just what you felt in the moment.

YOUR NEXT STEP:

Track every impulse purchase for the next seven days. Don't do it to judge yourself. Do it to learn. Writing a simple note beside each one that expresses how you felt, what pulled you in, can uncover more than you expect.

What's Next?

In Chapter 7, we'll move from reflection to design. You'll learn how to build a life-centered budget, a framework that balances your needs and wants, aligns with your priorities, and actually fits the way you live.

Designing a Life-Centered Budget

BUDGETING WITH PURPOSE

In Chapter 3, we talked about why most budgets fall apart. It's not usually about math it's about disconnection. People start tracking expenses without first asking what they actually want their money to support. That's why it often feels hollow or hard to stick with: it doesn't reflect real life or real priorities.

A life-centered budget begins from a different place. It asks: *What kind of life are you trying to build? What do you want your money to make possible?* For some, it's more freedom in daily life. For others, it's a sense of stability or the ability to care for the people they love.

Yes, you'll still need limits, but those boundaries serve a deeper purpose: to create space for the things that genuinely enrich your life. That could mean time with loved ones, taking on meaningful projects, or simply having the peace of mind that comes from knowing you're building something solid.

You don't need to track every penny. Instead, you set clear, steady guidelines strong enough to keep your choices aligned with the life you actually want to live.

A Budget Designed for Real Life

A life-centered budget is about balance the harmony that comes from using your money to serve your *whole* life. Not just your bills or your future, but also the everyday moments that make living worthwhile. It doesn't chase extremes. It simply asks: *How can your money support your present needs, your future security, and your daily joy without letting one outweigh the others?*

The framework is built around three key areas:

1. **Essential Expenses** – the non-negotiables. These are the foundations that keep your world running smoothly: rent or mortgage payments, groceries, utilities, healthcare, and transportation. These costs bring stability. Covering them gives you peace of mind and a secure base from which every other decision can grow.

2. **The Freedom Fund** – the money you put toward building the future you want. That might mean growing your emergency savings, paying off debt to unlock future income, or investing in long-term goals like home ownership or early retirement. This is what gives you more choice and flexibility down the road.

3. **Enjoyment Spending** – the part most budgets ignore or downplay. But this is where life happens *now*. These are the purchases and experiences that bring energy and meaning to your days: travel, hobbies, dining out, or simply the things that make you feel more alive. A life-centered budget doesn't treat joy as optional it makes space for it *on purpose*.

When you care for all three areas with intention, your budget becomes more than a plan it becomes a reflection of the life you want to live. One that protects your stability, builds your future, and leaves room for the present.

Why Does This Work?

The strength of this framework lies in a psychological shift from a mindset of deprivation to one of direction. Instead of thinking "I can't spend on that," the inner question becomes: "Where do I want my money to go?" It's a subtle change in language, but it alters the entire experience. Suddenly, it's not about guilt or constant restraint, it's about saying yes to what actually matters.

Take Tom, a high earner in his mid-thirties. He made well over six figures, yet he constantly felt anxious about money. Despite the income, he was living paycheck to paycheck. His spending was random and reactive, based on the assumption that if he just kept earning more, things would eventually sort themselves out.

But when he finally sat down to look at his finances, the problem became clear: most of his money was going toward things that brought no real joy. He had no Freedom Fund, no savings, no investments, no cushion. One emergency could have sent everything spiraling.

When Tom began using the Life-Centered Budget, the change wasn't instant, but it was steady. He started cutting back, not out of guilt, but because he wanted to redirect his money toward something real. He automated savings. Built a Freedom Fund. And made sure there was still room for joy. What he discovered stuck with him: wealth isn't just what you earn it's what you're building.

ALIGNING YOUR BUDGET WITH YOUR VALUES

A Life-Centered Budget only works if it reflects who *you* are. Start with a simple but powerful question: "Does my spending reflect what I truly care about?"

For Lisa, the answer brought clarity. She realized that her constant anxiety stemmed from not having a financial cushion. So, she redirected money from impulse purchases into an emergency fund and with each deposit, her peace of mind grew.

Nina, on the other hand, valued connection and travel. But when she looked closely, most of her income was disappearing into unused subscriptions and last-minute takeout meals. Once she saw the gap between what she valued and what she was funding, she made small changes that felt empowering, not restrictive.

This is the heart of it: if generosity matters to you, budget for it. If creativity matters, carve out space for the tools and time that bring it to life. When your money supports your values, you're no longer just spending you're building. And what you build is a life that feels aligned, intentional, and deeply your own. That's the real win.

When Values Clash – Making Tradeoffs Without Guilt

Sometimes the hardest part of budgeting isn't choosing between a want and a need it's choosing between two things you deeply care about.

Elena loved to travel. Exploring new places lit her up.

But she also longed to be debt-free. Her student loans had weighed on her for years, and trying to fund both dreams at once left her stretched thin. She wasn't traveling the way she wanted to, and her debt barely moved.

Eventually, she made a decision. For one year, she would pause her travel plans and focus every extra euro on paying off her loans. She still found joy in local adventures, but her energy was no longer split and that clarity brought her peace.

Your values won't always conflict. But when they are, don't see it as a failure.

See it as sequencing. You're not giving up on what matters; you're choosing what matters most right now. That's the purpose of a Life-Centered Budget: not to give you everything at once, but to help you focus your time, energy, and resources where they'll have the greatest impact in this season of your life.

Bridging Big Goals and Daily Spending

It's one thing to dream big, save for a down payment, take a bucket-list trip, or build a six-month emergency fund. But without anchoring those dreams to monthly decisions, they remain just that: dreams.

A Life-Centered Budget doesn't just capture your present; it bridges your everyday spending to your long-term goals. If you want to save $6,000 this year, that's $500 a month. Planning a $3,000 trip in December? That's $250 a month starting in January.

Breaking big goals into monthly contributions gives them a place to live inside your real life. It also reduces pressure. You don't need to "find" $6,000 at the end of the year; you simply need to follow the rhythm you've already set.

TRY THIS:
Pick one annual goal and reverse-engineer it into a monthly figure. Then add it to your Freedom Fund or assign it a custom category in your budget. Give your future a seat at the monthly table.

AUTOMATING YOUR LIFE-CENTERED BUDGET

One of the most effective ways to stay on track with your budget is simple: make it automatic.

Automation takes the pressure off. It builds consistency into your financial life so that progress continues even when your attention is elsewhere.

Back in Chapter 3, we talked about the *Psychology of Saving* and how the Set-and-Forget Method helps bypass decision fatigue by moving good habits into the background. That same principle applies not only here, it works across your entire financial system.

How to Put Your Life-Centered Budget on Autopilot:

Direct Deposit Allocation
If your employer allows it, split your paycheck automatically.

You might send 50% to your main account for Essentials, 30% to a separate "fun" account for Enjoyment, and 20% to savings or debt repayment for your Freedom Fund.

Your exact percentages will vary but the structure helps you stay aligned, without having to make that decision every month.

Automatic Transfers

Set up recurring transfers weekly, bi-weekly, or monthly toward your goals. Whether it's building an emergency fund, paying off debt, or investing for the future, consistency matters more than amount.

Small steps, repeated, compound over time.

Use Budgeting Apps

Apps like YNAB, Mint, or PocketGuard can help you monitor spending and spot patterns without the need to manually track every purchase. They're optional, but they can lighten the load and make budgeting feel more manageable.

TRY THIS:

Set up one small automated transfer today, just $10 a week into a savings or investment account. That single habit can create forward motion, reducing the effort it takes to stay on track.

THE JOY-BASED SPENDING PLAN

Joy-Based Spending is a simple but powerful idea: spend more on what truly matters to you. You can't control everything you spend on but you *can* choose to direct more of your money toward what truly matters, and less toward what doesn't. The goal is simple: fund joy on purpose, not by accident.

It starts with noticing what consistently brings you joy.

Take a moment to name the experiences, activities, or purchases that offer *real* satisfaction. These aren't always big or flashy. For some, it's travel. For others, it's quiet time with a hobby, treating someone they care about, or simply the comfort of having a financial cushion. The next step is to give joy a home in your budget.

That could mean setting aside a small monthly amount for weekend getaways, regular dinners with friends, or tools for a creative project. The details will be unique to you but the principle is the same: joy isn't extra it's essential. This approach works best when paired with quiet reflection.

Now and then, look back over your recent spending and ask yourself: Did this bring me lasting happiness? That one question can realign your habits more effectively than any spreadsheet ever could.

TRY THIS:
Choose one meaningful, joy-centered category like travel, creativity, or connection, and name it in your budget. Even a small recurring contribution can begin to shift your finances toward the life you want.

Life-Centered Budgeting on a Tight Income

It's easy to assume that intentional spending is only for those with financial breathing room. But when resources are limited, aligning your money with what matters becomes even more essential. A Life-Centered Budget is about making sure every dollar, no matter how small, contributes to your well-being in ways that count. Because, if every dollar matters, then where each dollar goes matters even more.

You may not have the flexibility to save large amounts or fund every priority right now. But you can still make small, thoughtful choices that reflect what you care about. That might look like:

1. Choosing groceries that let you cook one shared meal each week with someone you care about.

2. Shifting from impulse buys to a tiny weekly savings habit, even $5 a week adds up.

3. Making space in your budget, however small, for a low-cost ritual that gives you joy or rest.

When you're working with a limited income, the goal isn't to follow a perfect formula; it's to protect your energy, preserve your values, and build momentum, even in small ways.

This approach also sets the foundation for when your income grows. Because when that happens, you'll already have the tools and clarity to use new money wisely, rather than watching it disappear into unconscious spending.

STAYING FLEXIBLE WHEN LIFE DOESN'T GO TO PLAN

Even the most thoughtful budget will be tested by the realities of life.

That's not a flaw in your plan; it's proof that your plan needs room to breathe.

Start with the unexpected. Emergencies aren't rare they're just poorly timed. Whether it's a car repair, a last-minute flight, or an unexpected medical bill, these surprises tend to arrive just when things feel stable. That's why an emergency fund isn't just a financial tool; it's a psychological anchor. It gives you a sense of calm when life tilts sideways, it lets you respond with clarity instead of panic.

Then there's change that looks like progress. A new job. A raise. A bonus. It's easy to treat new income as a reason to upgrade your lifestyle right away. But if you can pause just briefly and reroute some of that momentum toward long-term goals or debt reduction, you build something deeper than comfort. You build freedom.

That doesn't mean saying no to enjoyment.

It means choosing *what kind of enjoyment* is worth building toward.

Social spending can be trickier. Sometimes it's planned: a trip, a celebration, a gift. Other times, it's a subtle dinner invite you don't want to turn down, a friend's shopping habit that starts to feel contagious. These moments can pull you out of alignment, not because they're wrong, but because *they weren't decided by you*.

One helpful habit is to pause and revisit your values. Ask not "Can I afford this?" but:

"Does this reflect the kind of life I want to create?"

And then, there are the quieter challenges. Fatigue. Burnout. The mental load of trying to stay on top of it all is overwhelming. Some months will just feel off and that's okay. The goal isn't perfection. It's direction. When things drift, return to your system with gentleness, not guilt.

Your budget isn't a punishment.

It's a flexible structure meant to support *you*.

When Life Changes, So Should Your Budget

Your budget isn't meant to stay the same forever. It's meant to evolve with you. A season of saving for a wedding might turn into one focused on starting a business. What mattered two years ago might no longer apply, and that's not a failure of discipline. That's growth.

Major transitions like becoming a parent, losing a job, moving to a new country, or facing a health shift, can completely upend your financial rhythm. But instead of trying to force an old plan to fit a new reality, let those moments be your signal to adapt.

Ask yourself:

- What are my new essentials?
- What brings me joy in this new season?
- What needs to pause, and what needs more support?

Emma, for example, became a single parent almost overnight. Her budget had to stretch. Essentials expanded, her Freedom Fund paused, and joy came from simple Saturday outings with her child. She didn't abandon her values; she redefined how to live them.

TRY THIS:
Think back to a time your financial rhythm was disrupted. What made it hard to stay grounded? Now consider one small system, habit, or boundary that might have helped. Write that down as something to test, not perfectly, but intentionally.

THE LONG-TERM BENEFITS OF A LIFE-CENTERED BUDGET

A Life-Centered Budget is a steady support, one that anchors your days, guides your choices, and makes them feel simpler. Life feels a little more manageable. And the impact goes far beyond your bank account.

You begin to notice a shift not just in your finances, but in your *state of mind*.

The mental noise around money the hesitation, the guilt, the urge to avoid starts to fade. Spending decisions feel calmer. You're not stuck in reactive mode anymore. You know where your money is going, and why. Clarity replaces anxiety.

Yes, your savings and investments grow. But what really expands is your *sense of room*.

Room to support someone else. Room to take a risk when it matters. That's the real meaning of financial freedom: not just having more, but needing *less panic* to face change.

A Life-Centered Budget adapts because life changes more often than we plan. Whether you're changing careers, raising children, or recovering after a setback, the system doesn't crack under pressure. It flexes. It holds. Because it's built around *your real priorities*, not just your bills, and that's what makes it strong.

But maybe the biggest shift isn't visible at all. It's the quiet, grounded feeling that your life actually fits you. That your days reflect your choices. That your money isn't just moving, it's moving in the direction of *what matters most*. And that's a kind of wealth no chart or tracker can ever measure.

TRY THIS:
Picture your life five years from now. Where are you living? How do your days feel? What are you free to do that you couldn't before? Write down three clear goals, and sketch out how your budget could become the bridge between here and there.

FINAL CHALLENGE: THE 30-DAY LIFE-CENTERED BUDGET EXPERIMENT

Here's a 30-day challenge to help you create a budget that works for you:

1. **Track All Expenses:** For the next 30 days, track every purchase, without judgment. Use a notebook, spreadsheet, or budgeting app.
2. **Identify Misalignments:** At the end of the month, review your spending. Where does it align with your values? Where does it fall short?
3. **Adjust and Automate:** Based on your findings, adjust your budget to better reflect your priorities. Set up automation to make the process easier.

Your Goal: By the end of the 30 days, you should feel more in control of your money and less stressed about finances. Budgeting should empower you, not limit you.

CLOSING THOUGHTS: BUDGETING = FREEDOM, NOT RESTRICTION

A Life-Centered Budget is about funding joy on purpose. It gives you clarity, reduces stress, and builds the confidence that comes from knowing your money is moving in the direction of what matters most.

When your spending reflects your values, budgeting becomes less about limits and more about choice.

YOUR NEXT STEP:

Make one small shift today. Reroute even a modest amount toward something meaningful: a goal, a joy, a priority. Let that small action remind you that you're in charge.

What's Next?

In Chapter 8, we'll move from managing money to protecting it. You'll learn how to build financial security through emergency funds, smart insurance decisions, and essential fraud protection strategies, so your progress stays protected, no matter what life throws your way.

Guarding Your Financial Future – Practical Steps for Security

INTRODUCTION: WHY FINANCIAL SECURITY MATTERS

Most people pour their energy into earning more or saving more. They track expenses, chase promotions, set bold goals, and work hard to grow. But far fewer devote the same care to *protecting* what they've already built.

The truth is, it doesn't take much to unravel years of progress, not because of one catastrophic event, but because financial strain often arrives in waves. A job loss might be manageable if it's the only problem. A medical bill could be absorbed if everything else is stable. But life rarely waits its turn. Sometimes, challenges collide: a layoff just as your car needs replacing. A health crisis while the markets are down and your investments are suddenly out of reach.

You might think: *I earn a decent income. I've made mostly smart choices. I don't overspend. I track my budget. I know what I'm doing.* And all of that may be true. But financial resilience isn't just about income or intelligence. It's about having *buffers* and *systems* in place for when multiple things go wrong *at once*.

Without that foundation, even high earners can find themselves scrambling pulling from long-term investments at a loss, taking on high-interest debt, or delaying plans they thought were already secure.

This is why protection matters. Not because we expect disaster, but because we respect reality. Its messiness. Its timing. Its indifference to how prepared we *feel*.

A strong financial safety net brings two gifts: steadiness now and readiness later.

It turns uncertainty into something manageable because you've already done the work to stay steady when life gets loud. So why do so many people skip this step?

One reason is a psychological blind spot called *normalcy bias*, our tendency to assume that tomorrow will look like yesterday. If nothing terrible has happened yet, we quietly assume it probably won't. That mindset feels safe in the moment, but it leaves us exposed. When we expect the future to echo the past, we don't build for the unexpected.

This chapter is about building that calm intentionally, step by step. You'll learn how to create an emergency fund that *actually works*, how to protect yourself from fraud and identity theft, and how to use insurance as a *strategic tool*, not just a formality.

These may seem like technical moves. But in truth, they're quiet acts of self-respect.

They're long-term thinking in action. And they ensure that the life you've built continues to serve you no matter what life throws your way.

THE 3 LAYERS OF FINANCIAL SECURITY

A strong financial foundation isn't just income and savings. It's a layered system. To truly protect your future, you need a multi-layered safety net. One that prepares you for sudden events, shields you from major loss, quietly guards against invisible digital threats, and gives you room to recover without starting over.

These four layers work together to keep your financial life intact when things go wrong:

1. Emergency Fund

This is your first line of defense. It's the cash you can access immediately when something breaks, falls through, or catches you off guard – a blown tire, an urgent dental procedure, or a gap between jobs. These aren't rare events. They're part of life, scattered across time, just waiting to show up. An emergency fund gives you breathing room when pressure rises. It keeps you from scrambling, from reaching for high-interest credit, or tapping into savings meant for your future. It's not just about the money, it's about the *moment*. The moment when calm matters most.

2. Insurance Protection

Some challenges are simply too large for any savings account to absorb: a sudden illness, a major car accident, a flooded basement, or an injury that keeps you from working for months. These aren't inconveniences. They're derailments. And they don't wait until you're ready. That's where insurance steps in. The right policies won't fix everything, but they create a buffer. They give you time, space, and stability in the very moments when clarity is hardest to find. Instead of scrambling to cover overwhelming costs, you get the chance to recover with less disruption. Insurance isn't a luxury. It's a quiet promise to your future self: *I'll be here for you, even in the worst-case scenario.*

3. Fraud and Identity Theft Protection

Digital threats are no longer rare or distant. They're constant and increasingly sophisticated. Today, your identity, account logins, and financial data carry as much value as the money in your wallet and can vanish just as fast.

A single weak password or compromised email can spiral into drained accounts, frozen cards, and months of frustration trying to reclaim what's yours. That's why protecting your digital life isn't just a tech precaution; it's a core part of financial security. Use strong, unique passwords. Turn on multi-factor authentication. Consider credit monitoring. Back up your important files. These aren't overreactions. They're basic hygiene in a digital financial world. Security is no longer optional. It's part of being prepared.

4. Legal and Document Safeguards

A crisis doesn't always give you time to prepare. Whether it's sudden illness, the unexpected death of a loved one, or a legal dispute, the difference between chaos and calm often comes down to one thing: Are your key documents ready? A power of attorney. A will. Clear insurance details. Account access info. Backup copies of your ID and financial records. These ensure that *you* or *your loved ones* can act without delay or confusion. Without them, even simple decisions can become stressful, delayed, or contested. This isn't just paperwork. It's foresight in action. And when life throws something hard your way, that foresight becomes a form of calm.

TRY THIS:

Take five minutes to audit your own setup. Do you have cash set aside for emergencies? Are your major risks insured appropriately? Is your online security strong enough to protect your financial identity? Choose one weak spot and make a plan to strengthen it this week.

BUILDING AN EMERGENCY FUND THAT LASTS

Your emergency fund is your financial shock absorber. It helps you stay grounded when Life jolts you with the unexpected. A flat tire. A sick child. A layoff you didn't see coming. And without a buffer, even a small disruption can derail your goals or plunge you into high-interest debt. Yet despite its importance, many people still struggle to build one. Studies show that a large percentage of households wouldn't be able to cover even a modest unplanned expense without borrowing.

Take Lisa Carter. You may remember her from earlier chapters, the one who realized her spending didn't reflect her values. After that wake-up call, she began cutting back on impulse buys and redirecting money toward what mattered more. But before that shift, Lisa used to say: I'll save later.

Then her car broke down. A $900 repair bill arrived out of nowhere. She had no emergency fund, so she reached for a high-interest credit card. It took months to pay off. And the damage wasn't just financial. It was emotional. The stress followed her to work, to bed, into conversations. That's when it clicked: not having an emergency fund had cost her more than money. It had cost her peace of mind.

That's the thing about emergencies: they don't just drain your account. They drain your time, your energy, your confidence. And they rarely arrive when you feel "ready."

So how much should you aim for?

Start with a clear, doable target. At a minimum, try to set aside enough to cover three months of essential expenses rent, groceries, transportation, insurance, and basic bills. That kind of buffer gives you room to breathe when life throws something your way. If you want deeper peace of mind especially in uncertain times, or if you're self-employed aim for six to twelve months. A cushion like that doesn't just protect you from hardship. It gives you freedom. The freedom to walk away from a toxic job. To take a risk. To rest.

Of course, building it won't happen overnight. That's okay. What matters most is consistency. Even $20 or $50 set aside regularly will add up. Automate it if you can. And don't think of it as money you're withholding from today. Think of it as a gift to the version of you who will need it most. That future version will thank you not just for the funds, but for the calm they bring.

TRY THIS:

Estimate your bare-minimum monthly essentials, just the costs you'd need to keep life running if everything else fell away. Multiply that number by three. That's your first emergency fund milestone. Set a goal to reach it over the next few months, and let that target guide how you adjust your budget or savings habits.

Where to Keep Your Emergency Fund?

Building an emergency fund is one thing. Protecting it so that it's truly available when needed is another key aspect. Where you store this money matters.

One of the most effective strategies is to keep your emergency fund in a separate bank or credit union, entirely apart from your everyday checking account. Why? Because accessibility can be a double-edged sword. If your emergency savings are just a swipe away, it becomes easy to justify using them for things that aren't emergencies, such as concert tickets, flash sales, or spontaneous weekend getaways.

That's why "out of sight" can mean "out of temptation." A separate institution creates a simple but powerful buffer. You can still access the money quickly when it's truly needed, but not so quickly that you'll tap into it on a whim.

Within that separate account, opt for a high-yield savings account (HYSA). These accounts typically offer better interest rates than traditional savings accounts, helping your emergency fund grow quietly in the background. And because HYSAs are liquid, your money stays easy to access, without the risk of being tied up in unpredictable investments.

One common mistake is trying to "grow" your emergency fund with stocks, crypto, or long-term bonds. These tools might have their place in your Freedom Fund or retirement strategy, but not here. In an emergency, the last thing you want is for your money to have dropped in value or to be stuck in something you can't access without delay or penalty.

The rule here is simple: your emergency fund should be safe, separate, and ready. If those three boxes are checked, you're not just saving you're preserving your peace of mind.

TRY THIS:

Calculate your essential monthly expenses: housing, groceries, transportation, insurance, and utilities. Multiply that number by three, six, or even twelve to define your emergency savings target. Then, open a high-yield savings account just for that purpose.

THE RIGHT INSURANCE FOR FINANCIAL PROTECTION

Insurance often gets treated like a chore. It's something you sign up for, pay for, and hope never to use. And it's no wonder. For many people, the word itself triggers a mix of confusion and resistance. We've all had that call from a persistent agent, pitching a policy we don't fully understand. Add in vague language, fine print, and a reputation that leans more toward hassle than help, and it's easy to see why people put it off sometimes until it's too late.

But when viewed correctly, insurance isn't a nuisance. It's a safeguard. For a relatively small cost, the right policy can shield you from rare but financially devastating events. It transfers the risk of the unpredictable like medical emergencies, car accidents, fire, theft, or injury, to a system designed to absorb it. Think of it as a quiet partner in your financial plan. You hope never to need it, but when you do, it can protect years of progress in an instant.

That said, not all insurance is created equal. And not everything in life needs to be insured. One of the most common traps people fall into is over-insurance. They pay for coverage that sounds comforting but delivers little value. Smartphone insurance, extended warranties on kitchen gadgets, or add-on protection plans at the checkout counter may seem smart in the moment, but often end up costing more than they're worth. Many of these micro-policies are built less to protect you and more to boost retailer profits.

Before signing up, ask yourself: Would this loss be truly disruptive or just inconvenient? If it's the latter, you may be better off self-insuring through your emergency fund.

To make smart decisions, get advice from the right sources. Independent financial advisors or consumer protection organizations can help you separate essentials from extras based on your life stage, obligations, and risk profile. Be cautious when the advice comes from someone who profits directly from the sale. And remember: urgency is rarely a sign of wisdom. If you're being rushed to "lock in a deal," step back. Read the details carefully, and reassess with a clear mind.

Insurance isn't about expecting disaster. It's about respecting uncertainty and being ready for it calmly and wisely.

Essential Insurance Categories to Consider:

Not every policy will apply to every person, and availability depends on your country, your income, and your public system. But some protections are nearly universal in their importance. Here are the ones worth pausing for and understanding.

Health Insurance

Unexpected medical costs can unravel your finances faster than almost anything else. One scan. One surgery. One overnight stay. Even in countries with public healthcare, the gaps, whether in coverage, speed, or specialist access, can be surprising. Supplemental plans can help reduce wait times, access private care, or cover out-of-pocket costs. If your body carries your ambitions (and it does), this is your first line of defense.

Disability Insurance

This one's often ignored until it's too late. If you rely on your job to pay the bills, you rely on your ability to work. But what if an accident, illness, or burnout makes that impossible? Disability insurance steps in to replace lost income, giving you time to recover without derailing everything else. Jason Patel skipped it, thinking he was too young to worry. After an injury, he spent six months watching his savings evaporate, proof that vulnerability doesn't ask for permission.

Life Insurance

If someone depends on you financially like a partner, a child, or even an aging parent, this isn't just about money. It's about continuity. It's about what happens in the silence after loss, when bills still arrive, when rent is still due, when a college dream still needs funding.

Money can't replace a person. But it can soften the weight of absence. It can keep your child in the same school. It can give your spouse time to grieve without also scrambling to cover the mortgage. It can prevent your parents from selling their home just to stay afloat. Life insurance isn't just a financial tool. It's a message you leave behind saying: I planned for you. A term life policy, especially when purchased young and healthy, is often surprisingly affordable. And yet its impact, if the unthinkable happens, can be the difference between crisis and resilience.

Homeowners or Renters Insurance

Whether you own your home or rent a single room, you've likely filled that space with the things that make life livable: furniture, clothing, electronics, and keepsakes. If those were suddenly lost due to fire, theft, or water damage, how quickly could you replace them?

Many renters assume insurance is just for property owners. But in reality, renters insurance protects everything you own within someone else's building. Landlords may insure the structure, but not your belongings. And replacing an apartment full of essentials, such as a laptop, bedding, cookware, and clothing can easily cost thousands, even if you live modestly.

The emotional impact of losing your home environment, especially in a disaster, can be overwhelming. Insurance doesn't erase the hardship, but it helps restore stability faster. It's not just about replacing objects; it's about regaining your footing with less stress, fewer delays, and minimal compromise.

The best part? Renters insurance is often inexpensive, sometimes costing less than a monthly streaming subscription. Yet it can offer thousands in protection and often includes liability coverage in case someone is injured in your space.

Car Insurance

Driving connects us to work, to loved ones, to daily life. But it also carries risk; one sudden moment can change everything. Car insurance is more than just a legal requirement; it's a financial safety net that protects you from the steep costs of accidents, damage, or injury on the road.

If you cause a crash, you could be held responsible for repairs, medical bills, and legal fees not just your own, but others' too. Without proper coverage, those costs can be financially devastating.

But even if you're not at fault, comprehensive and collision coverage can help repair or replace your vehicle quickly, so you're not left stranded or paying out of pocket. In many places, this kind of insurance also covers things like theft, weather damage, or collisions with animals.

It's easy to think, "I'm a careful driver; I probably won't need it." But that's the point, insurance steps in when control slips away. You don't need it until you desperately do. And when that time comes, it can save you from years of financial recovery.

In short, car insurance is one of those quiet agreements that lets you move through life with confidence, knowing that one mistake won't derail your finances.

(Optional) Umbrella Insurance

Most people think of insurance in terms of what they own, such as cars, homes, or health coverage. But umbrella insurance is about what you could lose in a lawsuit. It's an added layer of protection that kicks in when the limits of your standard policies (like auto or homeowners) aren't enough.

Let's say someone gets seriously injured on your property, or you're involved in a major accident with multiple claims. If the damages exceed your regular coverage, your savings, investments, or even future income could be at risk. That's where an umbrella policy steps in, covering the excess so you don't have to.

It's especially useful for people with higher exposure: landlords, public-facing professionals, freelancers, or anyone with meaningful assets to protect. But even if you're not wealthy, an umbrella policy can serve as a quiet shield against unpredictable, high-stakes situations. It's not mandatory, but for a relatively low premium, it offers reliable peace of mind. You may never need it, but if you do, it could be the one thing standing between a lawsuit and your long-term financial security.

Jason Patel learned this the hard way. He skipped disability insurance, telling himself, "I'm young and healthy. I don't need it." But then came a serious accident and six months of being unable to work. His savings drained faster than he imagined. What took years to build nearly collapsed in a matter of months. For just $20 a month, a disability policy could have fully replaced his paycheck and spared him the financial and emotional toll. That's the quiet power of smart protection: you don't notice it when life is calm. But when everything shakes, it's what holds you together.

TRY THIS:

Review your current insurance setup. Are you missing any essential categories? Are you paying for policies you don't truly need? If you're unsure, talk to a qualified financial advisor or a trusted nonprofit consumer agency. Aim to protect what matters without overpaying for what doesn't.

PREVENTING FRAUD AND IDENTITY THEFT

In today's connected world, protecting your financial life doesn't just mean guarding your bank account. It means protecting your identity, the digital version of you that lives in passwords, accounts, and online records. Cybercrime and financial scams aren't just headlines anymore; they're part of everyday risk, affecting millions of ordinary people each year.

And often, it doesn't start with carelessness. It starts with routine actions, such as clicking an email in a hurry, trusting a familiar logo, or reusing the same password one more time. It starts with what feels normal.

Greg never considered himself careless. He paid his bills on time, used online banking regularly, and considered himself reasonably cautious. But like many people, he didn't think much about digital security. He reused passwords. He clicked on links quickly when emails looked familiar.

One afternoon, he got an alert that looked like it came from his bank. The logo matched. The message was urgent: "Unusual login detected, please verify your identity." Without much thought, Greg clicked the link, landed on what looked like his usual banking login page, and entered his details.

The next morning, the real bank sent a text: "Did you just make a $3,200 purchase in Miami?" Greg hadn't been anywhere near Miami.

That link had been fake. The page had been fake. But the theft was real. Someone had used his login to drain his account, and the next six months were a blur of phone calls, paperwork, credit report corrections, and ongoing stress. He eventually got the money back, but the disruption lasted far longer than the fraud itself. His trust had been shaken.

Greg's story isn't rare. It's familiar. Because in a world where your data travels across dozens of platforms every day, protection isn't just about caution; it's about understanding where the risks lie and putting quiet systems in place to defend against them.

How to Protect Yourself from Fraud:

Staying safe from fraud doesn't require paranoia, but it does require a thoughtful, layered approach. You don't need to be an expert in cybersecurity to protect yourself; you just need a few well-placed systems, some regular habits, and a willingness to stay aware in an increasingly digital world.

One of the most effective steps you can take is to freeze your credit with the major credit bureaus. In the U.S., that means Experian, Equifax, and Trans Union. If you're elsewhere, check the equivalent agencies in your region. Freezing your credit doesn't affect your existing accounts or credit score, but it blocks anyone from opening new lines of credit in your name without your permission. That alone can stop many forms of identity theft before they begin.

Next, take a close look at the accounts you already use, especially those tied to your money, your identity, or your cloud storage. Use strong, unique passwords for each one. If remembering them all feels impossible, use a password manager. It's one of the best investments you can make in your security. And whenever the option exists, turn on two-factor authentication (2FA). This simple feature adds an extra step when you log in, like a code sent to your phone or app, but it makes it significantly harder for anyone else to access your accounts, even if they guess your password.

Being proactive also means keeping an eye on things. Make it a weekly habit to review your bank and credit card activity, even for small charges. The earlier you catch something unusual, the easier it is to resolve.

Another key area to watch is phishing scams, which are becoming more sophisticated. These aren't always sloppy emails filled with typos; some look nearly identical to official messages from your bank, a delivery service, or a government agency. Some even use cloned voices or highly personalized messages, pulled from public data, to seem eerily legitimate. The goal is always the same: to get you to reveal something, your password, your login code, or your banking information.

So here's the golden rule: if you receive a message asking for sensitive information, especially if it feels urgent pause. Don't click. Don't reply. Instead, contact the organization directly through a verified channel, like their website or customer service number, not the one listed in the message. Legitimate companies rarely ask for personal details over email or text, especially without prior notice.

Finally, when shopping online, use secure payment methods. Credit cards typically offer better fraud protection than debit cards and aren't directly linked to your checking account. That gives you more room to detect, report, and resolve unauthorized transactions if something goes wrong.

You don't need to do all of this at once. But small, steady actions can create a strong shield over time. Think of it as routine maintenance for your financial life, simple habits that help you move through the world with less worry and more confidence.

TRY THIS:

Sign up for a credit monitoring service, many are free or low-cost, and set up alerts for any new credit activity in your name. It's a small step that can give you an early warning if something goes wrong.

ESTATE PLANNING – SECURING YOUR LEGACY

Estate planning is often misunderstood. It can sound like something reserved for the ultra-wealthy or something to deal with only in old age. But in truth, it's one of the most grounded and generous steps you can take. It's an act of quiet stewardship, one that protects your wishes, reduces stress for your loved ones, and ensures that what you've worked for doesn't vanish into bureaucracy or confusion.

Even if you don't think of yourself as having "an estate," if you have bank accounts, a vehicle, digital assets, personal belongings, or people who depend on you, then estate planning matters. And it doesn't need to be expensive or overwhelming. A few clear steps can bring lasting clarity:

A Will

This is the foundation. A will outlines how your assets should be distributed after your death. Without one, the legal system makes those choices for you, often in ways that don't reflect your values or relationships. Creating a will is not morbid. It's loving. It provides structure during what is often a chaotic time, reducing disputes and confusion among family members who are already grieving.

Power of Attorney for Finances

If something unexpected leaves you unable to manage your finances- an illness, an accident, or even just temporary incapacity- this document ensures that someone you trust can step in without red tape. Bills still get paid. Important decisions aren't stalled. The chaos of a crisis doesn't spill over into your financial life. You can create one using a standard legal form, often available online or through a trusted advisor.

Beneficiary Designations

Some of your most important assets, like retirement accounts, life insurance policies, and investment platforms, don't follow the will at all. They follow beneficiary forms, often filled out years ago and forgotten. These forms override your will, so keeping them current is vital. After a major life event (marriage, divorce, the birth of a child), it's worth five minutes to review them. That small act could spare your loved ones months of legal sorting later.

(Optional) Trusts

Not everyone needs a trust, but in the right situations, it offers advantages that a will alone can't. A trust lets you skip probate, so assets transfer faster and with less friction. It allows you to guide how and when your money is used, especially important for minors or loved ones with special needs. It can also shield certain assets from taxes, lawsuits, or unintended exposure. And unlike a will, a trust remains private.

Legacy is a Kind of Love

You don't need to be rich to leave something meaningful behind. Estate planning isn't about wealth. It's about care. It's about making decisions now, while you're clearheaded and calm, so others won't have to make them in confusion or conflict later.

Legacy isn't just the money you leave. It's the peace you offer. If you own real estate, run a business, or care for someone who depends on you long-term, it's worth exploring. You don't need wealth to benefit from a trust, just complexity that deserves clarity.

TRY THIS:

If you don't yet have a will, make a commitment to create one this month. It can be simple. It can be updated later. But starting now will give you peace of mind, and give the people you love something even more valuable: clarity.

FINAL CHALLENGE: THE 7-DAY FINANCIAL SECURITY CHECKLIST

To implement these strategies, take on this 7-day challenge:

- **Save an extra deposit:** Contribute to your emergency fund (even $10).
- **Review or update insurance:** Ensure adequate protection.
- **Improve one security aspect:** Freeze credit, update passwords, enable 2FA.
- **Set up credit monitoring:** Track suspicious activity.
- **Start or review estate plan:** Protect legacy (wills, beneficiaries, POA).
- **Research ways to increase security:**
  Explore investments/savings strategies.
- **Reflect and set long-term goals:** Evaluate progress.

Your Goal: Build a bulletproof financial security plan that can weather life's uncertainties.

CLOSING THOUGHTS: FINANCIAL SECURITY = FINANCIAL FREEDOM

Building financial freedom means earning more, investing wisely, and protecting what you've already built. The savings you've grown, the choices you've made, the plans you've set in motion. These deserve to be safeguarded with the same care and clarity that created them.

Financial security is what helps those efforts endure. It cushions the blow of setbacks, keeps your progress on course through uncertain times, and gives you quiet confidence that your life can keep moving forward, even when life throws the unexpected your way.

YOUR NEXT STEP:

Pick one action to strengthen your financial foundation today. Review your insurance. Turn on two-factor authentication. Freeze your credit if needed. One thoughtful move is enough to start.

What's Next?

In Chapter 9, we shift gears and explore what financial freedom is really for. Because at its core, this journey isn't just about security or strategy. It's about joy. It's about meaning. It's about shaping a life that feels deeply worth living on your terms.

Rediscovering Joy Without Spending

THE MYTH THAT MORE MONEY = MORE HAPPINESS

By now, we've all heard it: "Money doesn't buy happiness." Not just once, dozens of times. It shows up in self-help books, podcasts, TED Talks, and well-meaning advice from people who seem to have it all figured out. But even after all that repetition, very little changes. The message rarely lands in a way that feels convincing.

It's one thing to hear the words. It's another to actually believe them, especially when life still feels like a race to catch up, or when joy seems tied to things we can see, hold, or afford. And let's be honest: that phrase hits differently depending on who's saying it. When someone wealthy says it, it feels detached, like they've already climbed the ladder and now want to pretend it didn't matter. The instinctive reply is something like, *"I'd rather cry in a Mercedes than on a bicycle."*

When someone who's struggling says it, it can sound like resignation. Either way, the listener tunes out. The idea gets dismissed not because it's wrong, but because it doesn't reflect how most people experience the world.

So maybe the point isn't to deny the link between money and happiness. Maybe it's to understand that link more honestly. To ask: What does money actually give us? What kinds of problems does it solve? And what are we hoping it will solve that it can't?

The research has been clear for years: after a certain level of stability when basic needs are met and life feels reasonably secure, the emotional return on extra income begins to flatten. In many cases, it even shrinks. That's not because people become ungrateful. It's because the things we hope money will fix, like boredom, insecurity, restlessness, or disconnection, aren't always financial problems.

So we try to patch emotional gaps with material solutions. And for a while, it works. But the relief doesn't last.

It's like pouring into a bucket with a slow leak. The thrill, the treat, the sense of arrival they never quite hold. So we keep topping it up, not realizing the hole isn't at the top. Over time, that cycle starts to feel normal. We don't just spend for pleasure, we spend for comfort, for belonging, for the feeling that we're making progress. And in doing so, we risk forgetting where joy actually lives.

Spending can still enhance life; no one's arguing otherwise. But the deepest forms of contentment rarely show up on receipts. They come from alignment. From living in a way that reflects what matters to you, even when no one is watching. The late-night laughter. The unnoticed win. The quiet satisfaction of doing something well, simply because it matters to you.

This chapter is about returning to that kind of fulfillment, the kind that doesn't begin with a purchase, but with attention, effort, and presence. Not to criticize spending, but to reconsider what it's been asked to replace. Many of life's most meaningful experiences cost little but ask more of us in other ways. And when we stop trying to buy joy and start learning how to participate in it, our relationship with money begins to shift. So does our sense of freedom.

THE SCIENCE OF HAPPINESS VS. SPENDING

What Really Makes People Happy?

Once we stop chasing happiness in the form of purchases, a deeper question emerges: What actually creates lasting well-being?

Positive psychology has spent decades exploring that question, and the findings are remarkably consistent. Over and over, research shows that deep happiness isn't about how much we have, but how we live. It's built quietly in the background of daily life through relationships, purpose, awareness, and participation, not through accumulation.

1. Strong Relationships and Social Connection

People feel most grounded when they feel connected. It doesn't require a large network or constant socializing, just a few relationships that feel steady, familiar, and real.

Happiness often shows up in quiet moments with people who truly see you. A friend who understands you without much explanation. A conversation that flows effortlessly. A shared silence that feels safe. It's not about being surrounded by people all the time. It's about knowing that someone's in your corner and that your presence matters to them just as much as theirs matters to you.

2. Purposeful Work and Meaningful Progress

Most people don't need a dream job. But they do need to feel that their time and energy count for something. That what they're contributing, whether it's care, craft, or quiet consistency, has real value.

That might look like raising a child, offering support, tending to something others overlook, or creating something new. These acts may not grab attention, but they carry weight.

And then there's the slow reward of getting better at something. Of learning, improving, sticking with it even when it's hard. That sense of progress, however small, can bring a steady kind of fulfillment that lasts far beyond the moment.

3. Gratitude and Mindfulness

Gratitude isn't about pretending everything is perfect. It's about making space to notice what's quietly good, the things you didn't ask for but are glad to have, the strength you forgot you had, and the parts of life that are working, even if others aren't.

Mindfulness works the same way. It's not about emptying your thoughts or performing calm; it's about being here long enough to notice what's real. A familiar sound. A kind gesture. The feel of warmth in your hands. These moments don't announce themselves. You only catch them if you're paying attention. And often, they're enough.

4. Physical and Mental Well-Being

When the body is depleted or the mind is stretched thin, even small joys can feel out of reach. It's hard to feel grounded when you're running on fumes.

Taking care of yourself through rest, movement, nourishment, and mental space isn't about chasing some ideal. It's about building the conditions for clarity and ease. A rested body thinks better. A calm mind sees more.

You don't need perfect routines or flawless health. You just need enough steadiness to move through the day with presence, not exhaustion.

TRY THIS:

Take a few minutes to reflect on what actually brings you joy. Write down three non-material things that make you feel alive, at peace, or fully yourself. It could be sharing a meal, laughing until your ribs hurt, walking under trees, or rereading a favorite book. Keep that list somewhere close, it's a compass pointing you back to the kind of fulfillment that doesn't come with a price tag.

HOW TO ENJOY LIFE WITHOUT OVERSPENDING

The things that make life feel rich and meaningful are often closer and simpler than we expect. They don't require a big budget or a special occasion- just a willingness to notice them, participate in them, and give them space in your life. It's about remembering that so much of what nourishes us deeply was never behind a paywall to begin with.

Spending time in nature, for example, offers a kind of peace that's hard to find elsewhere. A walk in a nearby park. A quiet trail. A windy beach. These moments don't require a ticket or a reservation, only your presence. They help you slow down, reconnect, and remember that joy can be as simple as fresh air and open sky.

Creative pursuits offer something similar. It's not about producing great art or hitting impressive milestones; it's about the quiet satisfaction of making something your own. Whether you're sketching in the margins, trying out a recipe from memory, learning a few guitar chords, or stitching something together with your hands, these small acts of creation bring a sense of grounding that lingers. And they're often more satisfying than anything you could buy.

Then there's the joy that lives in ordinary connection, the kind that comes from simply being with people you care about. Not just the obvious moments like celebrations or big events, but the smaller ones: cooking a simple meal together, laughing over an old memory, or staying up a little too late because the conversation kept going. These are the kinds of moments that build over time into something lasting. You don't always notice them as they're happening, but they become the texture of a life well lived.

Learning, too, can be its quiet joy. Not because you need it for your career or to be productive, but because curiosity is part of what makes us feel alive. Borrowing a book, diving into an unfamiliar topic, following an idea just because it's interesting. These are ways we stay connected to ourselves and to a sense of growth that doesn't rely on achievements or applause.

And sometimes, happiness arrives through the act of giving, not necessarily money, but through the quiet investment of your time, your care, or your attention. Checking in on someone. Offering to help. Sharing something you've learned. These gestures may seem small, but they carry a kind of meaning no purchase can replicate.

Spend Less and Live More

Lisa Carter, whom you met in earlier chapters, once believed that spending was the best way to enjoy life. For years, her idea of happiness was tied to weekend brunches, spur-of-the-moment purchases, and the small, fleeting highs that came with them. But as she began rethinking both her budget and her mindset, she decided to try something different. Instead of booking tables and splitting bills, she started hosting relaxed meals at home. These simple gatherings were filled with conversation, shared food, and a kind of warmth that couldn't be bought.

At first, cooking at home felt like extra work. There were groceries to buy, meals to plan, and the effort of coordinating with friends. But over time, something unexpected unfolded. Her friends began arriving not just as guests, but as participants bringing side dishes, a bottle of wine, or simply themselves. What began as a solitary effort gradually became a shared ritual, one that brought them closer in ways that felt deeply real. It saved them money, and the time spent together deepened their connection. The kitchen became more than just a place to prepare food; it became a space for companionship, a way of showing up for each other through food and the simple act of being there.

She also began trading hours of mindless online browsing for quiet hikes, community events, and slow weekends spent outdoors. Hiking, of course, came with its kind of unpredictability, mud, muscle aches, and maybe the occasional wrong turn. But the rewards ran deeper. Time in nature gave her space to clear her head in a way screens never could. Sometimes, she'd run into strangers who became familiar faces, small encounters that added a quiet kind of color to her weeks. What started as a way to "have fun without spending" gradually became part of her healing.

And what surprised her most wasn't how much she saved, but how much she gained. Presence, a quieter kind of joy, and the feeling that life could be deeply felt without being bought.

You don't need to overhaul your life to begin feeling more joy. But the next time you're tempted to spend just to feel something, pause. Ask yourself if there's already something around you or within you waiting to be noticed.

TRY THIS:

Plan one free or low-cost activity this week that brings you joy. Maybe it's a long walk with music in your ears. Maybe it's a phone call with someone who makes you laugh. Maybe it's trying something creative you haven't done in years. Then pay attention, not just to what you did, but to how you felt.

THE POWER OF GRATITUDE – APPRECIATING WHAT YOU HAVE

Modern life rarely invites us to notice what's already working. We're surrounded by reminders of what's missing, what could be better, what everyone else seems to have. In all that noise, gratitude can feel like a soft voice in the back of the room. But it's a steady one, and when we learn to hear it, it changes the way we move through the world.

Gratitude is a lens. When you start seeing what's good, your decisions begin to change. You don't reach for your wallet as quickly. You stop measuring your day in terms of what you've acquired and start noticing the small moments that give it shape: a warm meal you made yourself, a message that arrived at just the right time, the quiet click of something done not for recognition, but because it mattered to you.

One way to begin is with a simple gratitude journal. Each day, write down three specific things that felt good. A warm meal. A message from someone who knows you well. The quiet satisfaction of finishing something you started. These moments are small, but they anchor you. Over time, they create a sense of enough-ness that doesn't depend on spending.

You can also reach back. Think of a memory that made you feel whole, a walk that stretched past sunset, just because it felt good to keep going; laughter that came out of nowhere; an afternoon spent with no clock running, no pressure to be anywhere else. These moments didn't come with a price tag, but they stayed with you. That tells you something. It tells you that contentment often isn't bought, it's remembered, felt again, and rebuilt with intention.

In real time, you can practice the same awareness. When you feel the tug of wanting more, or the sting of comparison, ask yourself: *What's already here that's helping me carry today?* It might be your health, a hard-won insight, a friend who checks in, or your persistence. This isn't about settling. It's about noticing what's holding you up, even when life feels uncertain.

Gratitude doesn't mean pretending everything is fine. It means paying attention to what's quietly holding. That kind of awareness won't just help you spend more wisely it'll help you live more clearly. And over time, that clarity can do more for your financial well-being than any budgeting rule or spreadsheet.

TRY THIS:

Take one minute, right now, and write down something you're grateful for. A person, a place, a feeling, or a small detail that made your day better. Then ask yourself: Does this cost money? If not, notice how powerful that is.

FINAL CHALLENGE: THE 7-DAY NO-SPENDING JOY CHALLENGE

To put everything into practice, here's a challenge for you: For the next seven days, commit to finding joy without spending money.

Your Mission:

1. Day 1: *Enjoy a free activity.* Take a walk. Sit with a book. Write without a goal. Let the simplicity be enough for today.

2. Day 2: *Write down one thing you're grateful for.* Something small that steadied you, lifted you, or made the day feel more yours.

3. Day 3: *Skip the extras.* Let today pass without buying anything beyond what you need. Notice what urges come up, and what fades when you don't follow them.

4. Day 4: *Share time, not money.* Call someone. Visit. Cook together. Be with people who matter, without needing an occasion or a purchase to justify it.

5. Day 5: *Do something creative.* A sketch, a voice memo, a dish, a rearranged corner of your room. Creation as self-connection.

6. Day 6: *Give back.* Your time. A kind word. A helping hand. Offer something that costs nothing but carries weight.

7. Day 7: *Reflect.* Which moment stayed with you? What surprised you? Write down one thing that felt real, and why. That's the kind of wealth you can build on.

Your Goal: By the end of the week, you'll have a clearer understanding of where your happiness truly comes from. You might find that the things that make life feel rich were already within reach.

CLOSING THOUGHTS: TRUE WEALTH = MEANINGFUL EXPERIENCES

True wealth is found in how deeply you live. When you stop chasing joy through purchases and start noticing it in the moments already around you shared laughter, unguarded conversation something begins to shift.

You realize happiness was never waiting behind a screen or hiding at the bottom of a receipt. It's been here all along. And it grows quietly, steadily when you notice what's good, when you allow yourself to be known, when you carry even a small joy with care.

YOUR NEXT STEP

Choose one simple, low-cost or no-cost activity this week that brings you real joy. Maybe it's something you've been meaning to try. Maybe it's a quiet moment of connection with someone you love. Let that experience remind you: joy doesn't have to be bought it can be built.

What's Next?

In **Chapter 10**, we'll take this work even deeper. You'll explore what it means to fully own your financial story rewriting the limiting beliefs that shaped it and beginning to design a life that reflects who you are, not just what you can afford.

From "Can't" to "Choose" – Taking Ownership of Your Financial Story

INTRODUCTION: HOW MINDSET SHAPES YOUR FINANCIAL REALITY

For many people, money feels like something that *happens* to them. It's shaped by where they started, how they were raised, which doors were open and which ones weren't. Financial struggle often traces back to forces beyond our control: the economy, family expectations, missed chances, and a string of setbacks. These things matter. They shape the story.

But they don't have to write the whole thing.

At some point, the story we *inherited* becomes the story we *continue*. And while we can't choose what we were handed, we *can* choose how we carry it and what we build from it.

The beliefs we hold about money matter. What we think is possible, what we view as normal, what we believe we're capable of these quiet assumptions shape our choices. They act like an invisible script. If you believe you're bad with money, you may act in ways that reinforce that belief. But when you begin to see yourself differently as someone who can learn, grow, and adapt new choices start to emerge. Paths you once overlooked begin to feel possible.

That's the difference between *"I can't"* and *"I choose."*

One keeps the story closed. The other opens it.

Psychologist Carol Dweck calls this a growth mindset the belief that ability isn't fixed, but developed over time. When applied to money, a growth mindset is transformative. It means you can become someone who saves. Someone who invests. Someone who makes confident, thoughtful decisions not because you've always known how, but because you're learning how, one step at a time.

This chapter is about taking ownership of your financial story. It's about recognizing the role you're playing in that story right now and beginning to write the next part with more clarity and intention.

It all begins with paying attention to the beliefs that have been shaping your habits.

THE POWER OF FINANCIAL MINDSET SHIFTS

The way you think about money quietly shapes how you handle it.

Your thoughts influence your decisions, and your decisions, over time, shape your financial reality. If you've spent years believing that money will always be a struggle, it's easy to make choices often without realizing, that keep you stuck in that pattern. But when you begin to believe that change is possible, even in small ways, you start acting differently. You become more aware of your habits. Your choices feel less reactive, more intentional. And slowly, you begin to trust that learning is part of the process.

Here are a few common beliefs that often keep people feeling stuck and how you might begin to reframe them:

If you catch yourself thinking, "I'll never be rich,"

Try instead: *"I can learn to build wealth over time."*

Wealth doesn't have to mean extravagance. It's often built through small habits, steady decisions, and quiet consistency. You don't have to imagine yourself with millions just allow space for the idea that your financial situation can improve, and that you have an active role in that process.

If you think, "I'm bad with money,"

Reframe it as: *"I can get better at this."*

No one is born knowing how to budget, save, or invest. These are skills learned over time, shaped by practice. Mistakes aren't proof that you're hopeless; they're part of how you grow. The more you pay attention and stay curious, the stronger your instincts will become.

If you say, "I can't afford that,"

Try asking: *"How could I afford it, if it's truly worth it?"*

Not everything has to be within reach right now. But this question keeps the door open. It encourages creative problem-solving: Could you wait a little longer? Save gradually? Borrow, trade, or find an alternative path? The goal isn't to force an outcome it's to remind yourself that some things are worth figuring out.

TRY THIS:

Choose one financial belief that shows up often in your inner dialogue. Write it down exactly as it tends to sound in your mind. Then, rewrite it gently, without judgment, from a growth perspective. For instance, if you find yourself thinking, "I'll always be in debt," try: "I can create a step-by-step plan to reduce my debt and regain control." Small shifts in language can lead to big shifts in behavior.

REWRITING YOUR FINANCIAL STORY

The choices you've made with money whether careful, chaotic, or somewhere in between aren't life sentences. They're part of your story. They hold information and patterns. But they're not the whole of it. And if you're willing to look at them with honesty, they can teach you something useful.

Maybe you've taken on debt. Missed some opportunities. Spent without thinking. Avoided certain decisions because they felt too big to face. Those moments don't define your worth they simply reflect where you were and what felt possible at the time. Looking back isn't about rewriting the past. It's about understanding it, so you can make different choices moving forward.

Rewriting your financial story begins with reflection. Not harsh judgment. Not denial. Just a quiet look back: What choices helped you? Which ones made things harder? What patterns keep showing up?

Were some moments driven by fear, stress, urgency, or the need to prove something? This kind of reflection isn't about shame it's about clarity. You can't change the past, but you can learn from it. And learning is where real change begins. Every financial moment has something to teach you even the ones you'd rather forget.

Maybe you avoided building savings, and now you understand why it matters. Maybe you spent to feel seen, and now you're discovering healthier ways to feel whole. Even the choices that didn't serve you have value. Often, they're the ones that teach the most.

And then, gently, you begin to write the next chapter more deliberately. When old thoughts show up like I always mess this up or I'll never get ahead notice them. Then write something quieter and more useful beside them. Something like: I'm learning what works for me. I'm figuring this out, step by step. Let those words shape how you move forward.

TRY THIS:

Write a new financial identity statement; something that speaks to where you're going, not where you've been. For example: "I'm learning to build a healthier relationship with money. I make thoughtful decisions and take steady steps toward stability." Read it aloud. It might feel unfamiliar, even awkward. That's okay, you're letting a new version of the story begin to take shape.

THE "I CHOOSE" PRINCIPLE – TAKING CONTROL OF MONEY DECISIONS

One of the most meaningful changes you can make in your financial life is to start paying attention to how you describe your options especially the difference between saying "I can't" and "I choose."

At first glance, the words seem small. But they reveal something important about how you relate to the moment. Saying *"I can't"* often carries a quiet sense of defeat, as if the decision has already been made for you. Saying *"I choose"* reminds you that even within limits, even when the choices are difficult you still have agency. Naming them as yours changes how they feel. It reconnects you to the fact that you're involved.

This isn't about pretending things are easy or affordable when they're not. It's about being honest with yourself about your priorities. Instead of saying, *"I can't afford to go out,"* you might say, *"I'm staying in because I want to save for something that matters more to me."* That shift, subtle as it is, connects your current behavior to your deeper values. It doesn't take the difficulty away, but it helps you understand why you're making the choice.

Over time, this way of thinking reshapes how you see your money. Your budget starts to feel less like a set of rules and more like a reflection of what you care about. You stop seeing yourself as someone who's stuck. You start seeing yourself as someone who decides.

TRY THIS:

The next time you face a spending decision, notice your inner dialogue. If you catch yourself saying, *"I can't,"* pause. Rephrase it. Say, *"I choose."* For example: *"I choose not to spend on takeout this week, because I'm choosing to put that money toward my emergency fund."*

It's a small change in language, but it often shifts more than just the sentence. It changes how you feel about the decision. And over time, it changes how you see yourself.

HOW TO BUILD FINANCIAL CONFIDENCE

Financial confidence isn't something you're born with it's something you build.

It takes practice. It takes patience. It begins when you know just enough to try, and it grows when you keep going, even if progress feels slow. One small step, done consistently, can start to shift how you see yourself.

One of the most reliable ways to grow your financial confidence is by staying curious.

Read something that helps you make sense of a topic you've been avoiding.

Listen to a conversation that opens your perspective a little wider. Watch a short video that explains how savings work or how to make a budget feel less overwhelming.

You don't need to understand everything at once. Just keep chipping away at what feels confusing. Slowly, things that once felt out of reach begin to feel familiar. And that familiarity changes how you act.

Progress often shows up in quiet ways. Maybe you stuck to the spending plan you made.

Maybe you paused before an impulse purchase and chose differently. Maybe you opened your first savings account or set up an automatic transfer.

These aren't small moments. They're turning points. When you take time to notice them, you reinforce a deeper truth: you're changing. And that recognition helps you keep going.

The people around you matter, too.

If you're constantly hearing that discipline is pointless or that money is always chaotic, it's harder to stay with your process.

But when you're in conversation with people who are learning alongside you people who talk honestly about mistakes and growth it gets easier to keep your balance.

You don't have to do this alone.

You might find support in a local workshop, a friend with similar goals, or a financial educator whose approach resonates with you.

As we'll explore more deeply in Chapter 13, the people you spend time with shape not just your habits but your sense of what's possible.

TRY THIS:

Pick one small financial learning activity to try this week. It could be reading a few pages of a book, testing out a budgeting app, or listening to a podcast on money during your commute. Keep it simple and doable, something you can return to without effort.

FINAL CHALLENGE: THE 7-DAY FINANCIAL OWNERSHIP EXPERIMENT

For the next seven days, challenge yourself to take full ownership of your financial reality. Here's how:

1. *Identify and replace one limiting belief per day:* each day, write down a limiting belief about money and reframe it with a growth mindset.
2. *Make one conscious financial choice:* instead of reacting emotionally to spending decisions, pause and ask yourself, "What do I choose to do with my money?"
3. *Take one action toward financial confidence:* take a small step toward goals (budgeting, saving, researching investments).

Whether it's creating a budget, setting up automatic savings, or researching investment options, take one small step toward your financial goals.

Your Goal: take full ownership of your financial reality. By the end of the week, you'll have a clearer understanding of your financial mindset, a stronger sense of control over your money, and a plan for moving forward.

CLOSING THOUGHTS: YOUR FINANCIAL FUTURE IS IN YOUR HANDS

The most powerful truth in your financial life is this: you have more control than you think. When you shift from limitation to intention from *"I can't"* to *"I choose"*, you begin to reclaim that control in ways that truly matter.

YOUR NEXT STEP:

Pick one money habit to shift today. Maybe you start tracking what you spend. Cancel a subscription that's no longer useful. Set up a small automatic transfer into savings. Whatever it is, let it be simple, and let it remind you: you're not stuck.

What's Next?

In Chapter 11, we'll take the mystery out of investing: what it is, how it works, and why it matters. You'll learn the basics of stocks, bonds, and mutual funds, and gain a clear understanding of how investing fits into a long-term financial plan.

Investing Made Simple – Building Wealth Without the Overwhelm

WHY MOST PEOPLE AVOID INVESTING

Investing is one of the most powerful tools for building long-term wealth.

Yet for many, it's also one of the most avoided. It feels unpredictable. Intimidating. Like something reserved for experts, insiders, or people with money to lose.

In theory, we understand that investing helps money grow. But in practice, it often feels out of reach or unsafe. Not because people don't care about their future, but because somewhere along the way, investing came to feel like a risk they couldn't afford to take.

Sometimes, that fear comes from personal experience. Other times, it's inherited from parents or communities who saw investments go bad and never fully recovered. In those cases, hesitation isn't just confusion. It's protection. A shield against the kind of loss that leaves a mark.

The Stories We Inherit About Risk

Ryan knew that feeling well. He grew up in a family that had once been comfortably middle class. His grandfather had worked in finance and considered himself savvy with markets self-taught, sharp-witted, full of stories about outsmarting the system. For years, those stories seemed to hold true.

Ryan's childhood carried all the signs of financial ease: yearly trips to Florida, a visit to Disneyland when he was seven, birthday parties so full of gifts he didn't know where to start. He never thought of his family as rich, exactly, but they had enough. And enough felt secure.

Until everything changed. A market crash hit when Ryan was eleven, and his grandfather, who had managed most of the family's investments lost nearly everything. Retirement accounts, college savings, and even emergency funds were caught in the spiral.

But it wasn't just numbers disappearing on a screen. It was canceled plans. Growing tension. Fights behind half-closed doors that always came back to the same questions: how much had been lost, and why so much had been trusted to one man's certainty?

Within a year, the vacations stopped. Birthdays grew quieter. Then came the move to a smaller apartment and eventually, the divorce. No one talked openly about what happened. But the silence itself was loud.

Ryan could feel the weight of it in the way his mother flinched when bills arrived. In the way his father avoided eye contact during school meetings. In the way his grandfather, once so full of certainty, grew hollow and withdrawn. There was shame in the air, even years later.

Ryan never forgot what it felt like to lose the world he thought was stable. To go from rollercoasters and hotel pools to watching his parents argue over groceries. Somewhere deep inside, he internalized the message that investing was reckless. A gamble dressed up as strategy. And it destroyed families.

It didn't help that whenever investing made the news, it came cloaked in the language of crisis. Markets crashed. Fortunes vanished. Billionaires lost millions in a single afternoon. The headlines were theatrical and relentless: "Markets Tumble." "Wealth Wiped Out." The message was always the same: investing was dramatic, dangerous, and unpredictable.

No one wrote stories about the quiet investor who built wealth slowly, without noise or spectacle. That kind of patience didn't sell.

So Ryan chose what felt safe. He kept his money in a savings account: low return, low drama. There were no crashing charts. No chance of losing what little he had. It wasn't exciting, but it gave him a sense of calm he hadn't felt since childhood. And for a long time, that was enough. But as the years passed, that stillness began to shift. It no longer felt like safety. It started to feel like stagnation like standing still while the world moved on without him.

That's where he was when he ran into Marcus, an old friend from high school. They hadn't talked in a while, but decided to catch up at a quiet café on a Saturday morning.

Marcus had grown up in a different kind of household. His family didn't have much, and they didn't trust banks let alone the idea of investing. Money was something you kept close: in jars, under mattresses, or in envelopes around the house. They used what they had to get by. No one talked about building wealth.

But over time, Marcus got curious. He didn't have anyone to show him the ropes, so he figured it out himself. He read articles, listened to podcasts, watched videos, and asked a lot of questions even when it was uncomfortable. What he found surprised him. Investing wasn't some mysterious system for rich people. It was a tool. And if he took it seriously, it could help him build something better for the future.

Over coffee, Marcus asked Ryan a simple question: "Do you know what happens when you don't invest?" Ryan shrugged. "I don't lose money?" Marcus smiled. "Maybe. But you're definitely losing wealth."

That line stuck with Ryan. He had always believed he was protecting himself from risk. But somewhere along the way, that protection had hardened into avoidance. And now, he was beginning to see the cost through inflation, missed growth, and lost time. He wasn't avoiding risk anymore. He was guaranteeing loss, one quiet year at a time

Some people stay away from investing because they've been burned before, by market crashes, confusing products, or promises that didn't deliver. Others feel shut out by the jargon or assume it's something reserved for people with extra money or special knowledge. But behind all the noise, the core truths are surprisingly simple:

- **You don't need a lot of money to begin.**
  Many platforms let you start with as little as $10. The key is consistency.
- **You don't need to master everything before you begin.**
  A few clear principles are enough to get started with confidence. You'll deepen your understanding as you go, and

that steady learning, paired with consistent action, is what builds long-term success.

• **Your money can grow while you focus on other things.**
With a simple, well-structured plan, investing can become a quiet but steady engine in the background of your financial life.

This chapter breaks down what investing actually is, how to begin, and how to build a strategy that suits you. You'll learn the same essentials that helped Ryan shift from hesitation to momentum. And by the end, you'll be able to take your first step toward long-term financial growth.

UNDERSTANDING HOW INVESTING WORKS

Before diving into the how, it helps to understand the why.

At its core, investing is about transforming money from something that simply *sits* into something that *works*. Instead of letting it rest passively, you give it a purpose: to grow, to generate income, to build something meaningful for your future and to gradually reduce the financial burden on your shoulders.

That growth comes from placing money into assets designed to increase in value over time things, such as stocks, bonds, or real estate. When done thoughtfully, investing isn't just about making money. It's about shifting from *holding wealth* to *building it*.

Investing = Making Your Money Work for You

Saving matters. It's the foundation of financial security. But over the long run, saving alone often isn't enough to build meaningful wealth. That's because money sitting in a low-interest account usually grows too slowly to keep up with inflation. Investing, by contrast, gives your money the potential to grow faster, by owning pieces of things that gain value or produce income over time.

Even small investments can make a difference, especially when you give them time to work.

Compound Interest is Quietly Powerful

Often called the "eighth wonder of the world," compound interest is what happens when your investments earn returns, and then those returns begin earning returns.

The German word for it is Zinseszins, which translates directly to "interest on interest." It's a more precise term than we often use in English, and somehow captures the idea more cleanly: growth layered on top of growth, quietly building over time.

Here's how it works: if you invest $1,000 and it grows by 7% in a year, you'll have $1,070. The following year, that same 7% applies not just to your original $1,000, but to the full $1,070, bringing you to $1,144.90. The increase keeps building, not because you've added more, but because your past returns are doing part of the work.

Risk and Reward Go Hand in Hand

No investment is completely risk-free. That's part of the tradeoff. In general, the potential for greater reward comes with more ups and downs along the way.

Take stocks, for example. Historically, they've offered stronger long-term growth than bonds but in the short term, they can swing sharply. Prices rise and fall based on many factors: company performance, interest rates, headlines, even public mood. That movement is part of what gives stocks their long-term power, but it can feel chaotic if you're not prepared for it.

That's where diversification comes in. When you spread your money across different types of investments stocks, bonds, sectors, even global markets you're not trying to eliminate risk. You're managing it. Diversification doesn't mean everything moves in opposite directions. It means everything doesn't move the *same* way, at the *same* time, for the *same* reasons. And that kind of variety can help cushion your portfolio when parts of the market are under stress.

TRY THIS:

Look up one investing term today, something simple like index fund, compound interest, or asset allocation. Understanding these core ideas builds the foundation for long-term confidence.

THE BEST INVESTMENT STRATEGIES FOR BEGINNERS

You don't need to be an expert or wealthy to start investing. In fact, some of the most effective strategies are simple, low-cost, and designed for regular people who want to build steady, long-term growth. Here are approaches that work especially well for beginners, particularly within the U.S. financial system:

1. Index Funds and ETFs

Index funds and exchange-traded funds (ETFs) let you invest in the broader market, rather than trying to pick individual stocks. For example, an S&P 500 index fund gives you a small share of 500 large

U.S. companies in a single investment. It's a quiet, effective way to participate in overall market growth without needing to follow the news every day.

This approach gives you:

1. Built-in diversification, which helps reduce risk.
2. Simplicity, no need to analyze individual companies.
3. Access to long-term market growth with low fees and minimal upkeep.

2. Retirement Accounts (401(k), IRA, Roth IRA)

Retirement accounts are one of the most powerful ways to invest for the long haul. A 401(k), often offered through employers, and IRAs (including Roth IRAs), which you open individually, come with special tax benefits that help your investments grow more efficiently over time.

These accounts offer:

1. Tax advantages that can significantly boost your returns.
2. A natural structure for long-term, consistent investing.
3. In some cases, employer matching, essentially extra contributions you don't have to earn twice. If that's available to you, it's worth taking seriously.

3. Dollar-Cost Averaging (DCA)

Dollar-cost averaging means investing the same amount at regular intervals: weekly, monthly, or with every paycheck, regardless of what the market is doing. Instead of trying to time your investments perfectly, you focus on consistency.

This method helps you:

1. Avoid the stress of trying to guess market highs or lows.
2. Stay calm during market swings, because your plan doesn't change.
3. Build a steady habit of investing, which often matters more than perfect timing.

TRY THIS

If you haven't already, open a simple investment account, many apps make it easy to start. Set up a small automatic transfer, even if it's just $10 or $25 a month. What matters most is building the habit.

AVOIDING COMMON INVESTING MISTAKES

Even with a solid foundation, many people find themselves quietly sabotaging their investing journey, often without realizing it. The good news? Most of these mistakes are both common and preventable. Recognizing them is the first step toward a calmer, more confident investment experience.

1. Trying to Time the Market

It's natural to want to buy low and sell high. Whether it's stocks or real estate, the idea of perfect timing feels logical catch the rise, dodge the fall. Everyone dreams of buying just before prices soar or selling right before they dip. But in practice, market timing is rarely that clean and often misleading.

Even in real estate, the logic sounds appealing but tends to fall apart under real-world pressure. Transaction costs, unpredictable timelines, local shifts, and holding expenses all make precise exits hard to pull off. Most successful real estate investors don't build wealth by flipping at the perfect moment. They build it by holding over time, managing risk, and letting value grow steadily.

The same holds true in the stock market. Prices move fast and often without warning. Stepping out during uncertain times may feel like protection, but it often backfires. A handful of the strongest market days account for a large share of long-term gains and those days typically come right after the worst ones. If you're waiting on the sidelines for perfect timing, you risk missing the very moments that drive your growth.

Success doesn't come from guessing the best day to get in or out. It comes from staying in, with patience and a plan, so the full story has time to unfold.

2. Investing in Things You Don't Understand

It's easy to get swept up in the buzz about cryptocurrencies, meme stocks, or so-called "safe havens" like gold. And in today's world, the pitch often comes from people we trust. They sound confident. They speak your language. They show you charts and tell stories that feel eerily familiar: governments are printing money, the system is broken, and gold has always held its value. It feels smart to follow their lead.

But here's what often happens behind the scenes: someone shows you a chart of gold steadily rising over the past decade. They talk about inflation, instability, and the collapse of fiat currency. You nod along. It makes sense. Then they offer to sell you gold but not at the market price. They add a premium. A markup that quietly eats into your return before you've even begun. You end up paying far more than the asset is worth on the open market, often without realizing it.

This doesn't mean gold is bad. It means the way it was sold to you wasn't built on your understanding it was built on your fear. And that's exactly what makes it so tempting, and so risky.

You don't need to be an expert to start investing. Many people begin with something simple, like an index fund that tracks the S&P 500, without knowing every technical detail. That's okay. What matters is that the investment is built on sound principles, fits your time horizon, and supports your real goals.

The real danger starts when enthusiasm replaces clarity when trust in a person or narrative leads you to skip the due diligence. Especially in emotional moments fear of economic collapse, or a strong desire to "finally build wealth", it's easy to act fast. But investing well isn't about speed. It's about alignment: between your choices and your understanding.

Influencer culture has blurred the line between personality and expertise. When someone you like, admire, or relate to starts talking about investing, it's easy to let your guard down. But liking someone isn't the same as verifying their advice. Emotional connection can disguise high-risk suggestions as casual tips.

We're most vulnerable to poor financial decisions when the advice comes from people we already trust because we stop asking questions. We assume they've done the homework. We mistake their confidence for our own readiness. But your money deserves more than borrowed certainty.

It's okay to respect someone and still reject their investment advice.

It's okay to admire someone's mindset and still say, *"This isn't right for me."*

Start simple. Choose clarity over charisma. Spectacle might catch your attention, but it's stability that builds your future. Understand what you're investing in even at a basic level. Then let your knowledge and confidence grow, one calm, thoughtful decision at a time.

3. Panic-Selling During Downturns

Markets go up and down that's always been part of how they work. But when a downturn hits, it rarely feels normal. It feels personal, urgent, and loud. Headlines sharpen. The mood shifts. Even the most patient investors begin to second-guess their choices. In those moments, selling can seem like the only way to regain control. You might feel like you're protecting yourself by stepping out before things get worse. And for a while, that decision might bring relief. A break from the emotional weight of watching numbers fall.

But what often gets overlooked is what happens next. Recoveries don't wait for your comfort. They don't send a signal that it's safe again. In fact, some of the strongest days in the stock market often come right after the worst ones. And if you're not invested when those rebounds happen, the long-term cost can be significant. That's not just theory it's what the data shows, again and again.

Take the S&P 500, for example. From January 1, 2002, to December 31, 2022 a full 20-year period covering 5,036 trading days if you had simply stayed invested throughout, your money would have grown at an average annual rate of just over 9%. But if you missed only the 10 best days in that entire span just 10 out of 5,036 your return would have been cut nearly in half, dropping to around 5% per year. Miss the 20 best days, and it drops to about 2%. Miss the 30 best days, and your total return over two decades would have been nearly wiped out, landing close to zero.

This becomes even more critical if you're relying on your investments for income, such as during retirement. Withdrawing during a downturn hurts more than just your balance it reduces the capital you have left to recover with, and compresses the timeline for recovery itself. This timing risk, known as the sequence of returns risk, can have lasting effects. Losses early in retirement, especially when paired with withdrawals, can permanently reduce the size and resilience of your portfolio.

And yet, the impulse to sell rarely forms in isolation. It grows inside an emotional bubble shaped by news cycles, social media, friends, and trusted voices all reacting at once. During times of uncertainty like trade wars, elections, or global crises fear doesn't just emerge; it multiplies. And when enough people act on it, their behavior starts to feel like proof that panic is the right response. But history tells a different story. Over and over again, it offers a quieter, more consistent truth: the market has always recovered often sooner than expected.

That's why a steady, thoughtful plan matters. Not because it shields you from every loss, but because it protects you from turning temporary setbacks into permanent mistakes. A diversified portfolio, a long-term view, and the discipline to stay the course when emotions are loud these are your real safeguards. The most successful investors aren't the ones who never feel anxious. They're the ones who know that patience and perspective are more powerful than prediction.

As the saying goes: *"Time in the market not timing the market is what builds real wealth.*

This is why panic-selling isn't just emotional it's expensive. The market doesn't notify you when it's about to recover. It turns quietly, often when most people still feel uneasy. And if you're not there when it happens, you don't get the benefit. Staying invested even through discomfort is how long-term returns are earned.

That's also where the internet-born phrase *"diamond hands"* captures something unexpectedly wise. Beneath the jokes and memes lies a useful mindset: the ability to hold firm under pressure. In investing, that mindset matters not as a symbol of defiance, but as a sign of discipline.

Having diamond hands doesn't mean ignoring risk or refusing to think. It means knowing what you own, why you own it, and being willing to hold through turbulence because you have a plan. The investors who build real wealth aren't the ones who never feel fear. They're the ones who feel it but don't let it drive the wheel.

When you stay invested with purpose, even when the noise is loud, you give your portfolio the one thing it needs most: time. And over time, it's not the panic moves that shape your outcome. It's the quiet conviction to stay the course.

> **TRY THIS:**
> Commit to holding your investments for at least five years. This will help you avoid the temptation to panic-sell during market downturns.

4. Paying High Fees for Actively Managed Funds

For many high earners such as, doctors, entrepreneurs, and athletes, it feels only natural to delegate financial decisions to professionals. If your schedule is packed and your expertise lies elsewhere, why not hire someone whose job is to manage money? It seems responsible. Even smart.

But that well-meaning instinct often leads to high-cost, actively managed funds that promise personalized attention and market-beating performance. These funds come with higher fees, and their managers are skilled at highlighting the wins. Beneath the surface, though, the story is often different. While their track records may look impressive in short bursts, most actively managed funds lag behind simpler, lower-cost alternatives like index funds when measured over years. And those higher fees, even when they seem small, compound quietly, eating away at your gains. Over decades, that can cost you thousands or even tens of thousands of dollars.

For those without high incomes, the hesitation often looks different. You may feel unqualified, unsure where to start, or afraid of doing it "wrong." That's understandable. But the real challenge usually isn't ability, it's access to clarity. And here's the truth: you don't need to be wealthy or a financial expert to invest well. Simplicity and consistency still outperform complexity and hype.

If you do want professional help, look for a fiduciary financial advisor someone who is legally obligated to act in your best interest. Even better, seek a fee-only advisor, paid directly by you not through commissions or product sales. These professionals do exist, and they can offer real value, especially when their incentives align with yours.

The key takeaway? You don't need perfect knowledge. You need clear intentions, long-term thinking, and a structure that supports not exploits you. Whether you invest independently or with guidance, the principles remain the same: keep costs low, diversify broadly, and give your investments time to grow. This approach has worked for millions of people, across generations and market cycles.

Of course, no strategy is without critics. Some experts worry that the rise of passive investing may distort markets channeling more money into large companies simply because they're in the index, not because they're well-valued. It's a fair point, and worth keeping in view.

But for most individual investors especially those early in the journey these macro concerns don't change the core truth: a simple, diversified, long-term approach still offers the clearest path to sustainable wealth. You don't need perfect timing. You don't need secret insights. You just need patience, clarity, and a steady hand.

HOW TO MAKE INVESTING AUTOMATIC

One of the most powerful advantages you can give yourself as an investor is consistency. But consistency is hard when life gets busy, markets get noisy, or your confidence wavers. That's why automating your investments isn't just convenient, it's one of the smartest decisions you can make. It protects you from your own doubts, removes the temptation to tinker, and builds wealth quietly in the background.

Step 1: Automate Your Contributions

If you've already set up a retirement account like a 401(k) through your employer or an IRA you're off to a strong start. These accounts offer powerful tax advantages, as we've discussed. But the real magic begins when you automate your contributions. By scheduling automatic deposits ideally timed with your payday you turn investing into a habit, not a monthly decision to revisit. That consistency keeps you on track, even when markets wobble or life gets chaotic.

Already contributing to a 401(k)? Great, see if you can increase your contribution rate by 1–2%, or make sure you're getting the full employer match if one is offered. Many people leave money on the table by not contributing enough to receive the full match.

Using an IRA? Set up a recurring monthly deposit that fits your current budget, even if it's small to start. The point isn't perfection. It's progress. You can always increase it later as your financial comfort grows.

Step 2: Reinvest Your Dividends Automatically

Most investment platforms and funds let you opt into dividend reinvestment, commonly known as a DRIP (Dividend Reinvestment Plan). Instead of receiving dividend payouts as cash, your dividends are automatically used to purchase more shares of the same investment. This small adjustment can significantly accelerate the compounding process. Over time, reinvested dividends can account for a surprisingly large portion of your total returns especially in broad-based index funds.

Step 3: Stop Watching the Market Every Day

This one can feel counterintuitive. Shouldn't you keep a close eye on your money? In reality, checking too often does more harm than good. Market dips, corrections, and emotionally charged headlines are a normal part of the journey but long-term investing isn't a spectator sport. It's a discipline. The more frequently you watch, the more tempted you'll be to react emotionally and disrupt an otherwise sound plan.

A better approach? Check in every few months or even just once a year to review your progress, rebalance if necessary, and make any small adjustments. The rest of the time, let your system do what it's designed to do: quietly work in the background while you focus on living your life.

> **TRY THIS:**
> Choose a low-cost index fund, open an account, and set up a small automatic contribution, say $25 or $50 per month. Then turn on dividend reinvestment. Let time and consistency do the rest.

FINAL CHALLENGE: THE 30-DAY INVESTMENT CONFIDENCE PLAN

To help you take the first steps toward investing success, here's a 30-day plan to build your confidence and get started:

- *Learn one investing concept per week:* spend the next four weeks learning about key investing concepts like compounding, asset allocation, index funds, and dollar-cost averaging. This knowledge will give you the foundation you need to make informed decisions.
- *Open and fund an investment account:* even if you start with just $10, opening an investment account is a crucial first step. Choose a platform that aligns with your goals and offers low-cost investment options.
- *Set up an automatic investing habit:* set up a recurring deposit (even just $10) and reinvest your dividends to ensure consistent growth. Over time, these small actions will add up to significant wealth.
- *Review your progress and adjust your goals:* take time to reflect on your journey, evaluate where you are, and make any necessary adjustments to your investment strategy.

Your Goal: Build confidence in investing and take action toward long-term wealth. By the end of the 30 days, you'll have a solid foundation and a clear plan for the future.

CLOSING THOUGHTS: INVESTING IS FOR EVERYONE

You don't need to be an expert to be a successful investor. What matters most isn't flawless knowledge it's consistent, intentional action. Please keep it simple by choosing low-cost index funds and ETFs. They offer broad diversification, minimal fees, and a strong track record of reliable performance. Stay consistent by investing regularly, even when the market feels uncertain. In the end, it's not prediction that builds wealth, it's discipline.

And above all, think long-term. Real growth takes time. Let compounding do its quiet work. Resist the urge to react to every headline or downturn. Stay the course, and let time work in your favor.

YOUR NEXT STEP:

Take one small action today: open an account, set up a recurring deposit, or learn one new concept. Every investing journey starts this way, not with a bold leap, but with a clear, quiet step in the right direction.

What's Next?

In Chapter 12, we'll shift from building wealth to using it well. You'll discover how giving with purpose, whether through time, resources, or generosity, can multiply your impact and help shape a life of deeper meaning.

Giving With Purpose – Aligning Charity With Your Values

INTRODUCTION: WHY GIVING MATTERS

Giving is often something we imagine doing "someday" after the debts are paid, the savings goals are met, and life feels a little more secure. It's framed as a bonus, a gesture for holidays or windfalls, not a regular part of a financially healthy life. But true financial freedom isn't just about what you're able to keep. It's also about what you're free to let go of. Purposeful giving doesn't just support others it reflects the values that make wealth meaningful in the first place.

Still, the instinct to give often runs into quiet resistance. For many, it's the feeling of scarcity the belief that generosity is only for people who've "made it." Giving feels like a luxury, not a pathway to deeper wealth.

Other times, it's guilt. We give from pressure or obligation, not conviction. And when generosity becomes duty, it loses its power to nourish.

Sometimes, it's simply disconnection. We donate but never see what changed. That lack of visibility can make giving feel hollow, slowly silencing the desire to give again.

THE SHIFT: FROM OBLIGATION TO ALIGNMENT

Purposeful giving changes everything.

It turns charity from a vague obligation into a deliberate, fulfilling act. When your giving aligns with your deepest values whether that's education, justice, health, climate, or faith it shifts from something you *should* do to something you *choose* to do. It becomes less about how much you give, and more about how clearly and intentionally you give.

You might remember Sophia Ramirez from Chapter 3 the one who discovered that even small amounts, handled with consistency, could create real impact. For years, she told herself that giving wasn't realistic: *"I'll give when I have more."* Her financial goals felt too urgent, her future too uncertain. Even when she wanted to be generous, a quiet voice always asked, *"Does a small donation even matter?"*

She wasn't indifferent. She just didn't feel ready. Like many people, she assumed generosity was something to delay until the debt was paid off, the savings account was full, the future felt secure. But one day, she read a short story about a $50 donation that provided school supplies for an entire classroom. That number stuck with her not because it was large, but because it was *enough*. Enough to help. Enough to shift her perspective.

Sophia had already seen how small actions could create momentum she experienced that when she first automated her savings. But this was different. This was about choosing to give *before* everything felt settled. And realizing that readiness isn't about having more it's about deciding to start. That moment didn't make her wealthy. But it made her generous. Not out of guilt. Not out of surplus. Out of clarity. Giving became part of how she lived not because she had to, but because she could.

This chapter will help you explore how to align your giving with what truly matters to you, so it's not just generous, but grounded in purpose. We'll look at how to give in ways that feel meaningful, not obligatory empowering, not performative. Because in the end, giving isn't only a financial choice. It's a mindset shift. One that has the power to transform not just the lives you touch, but your own.

INTENTIONAL GIVING: WHY IT MATTERS

Generosity isn't just a transaction it's a decision that can transform both the giver and the recipient. When done with intention, giving becomes more than an act of kindness; it becomes a powerful tool for personal, emotional, and even financial growth.

Psychologically, giving is deeply rewarding. Research shows that acts of generosity activate the brain's reward centers and release endorphins producing what's often called the "helper's high." This small but powerful neurological boost creates a positive feedback loop: giving feels good, so you're more likely to do it again. Over time, consistent generosity has been linked to greater happiness, lower stress, and a stronger sense of purpose especially in a world that so often pulls us toward anxiety and isolation.

Giving also deepens your connection to others. When you support causes you care about whether through money, time, or attention you become an active participant in shaping your community or the wider world. That engagement fosters a sense of belonging and emotional resilience, both of which are closely tied to long-term well-being.

It can even reshape how you think about money. Generosity reinforces an abundance mindset. Rather than fixating on what you lack, it affirms that you have enough to share. That single shift from scarcity to sufficiency can transform your financial outlook, helping you see wealth not just as a number, but as a source of meaning, agency, and contribution.

And while it shouldn't be the reason you give, there are often practical benefits too. In many countries, charitable donations can reduce your taxable income, making generosity more sustainable. The tax break doesn't lessen the meaning it simply helps giving become part of your long-term financial plan.

Beyond the individual, generosity creates tangible impact on a societal scale. Charitable contributions fund medical research, expand access to education, provide disaster relief, and drive systemic change. The effects are amplified when people act collectively what no one could accomplish alone becomes possible through shared generosity.

Consider the global response to natural disasters. Donations enable the rapid delivery of food, shelter, and medical care to those in crisis. But the impact doesn't stop there. Over time, these contributions help rebuild stronger, more resilient communities. Giving doesn't just address immediate needs; it plants seeds of long-term hope.

TRY THIS:

Write down a cause or issue you care deeply about. Even a single word or phrase is enough. This small act of reflection can clarify your values and begin shaping a giving practice rooted in intention, not pressure.

Sophia's Turning Point

The $50 classroom story stuck with Sophia. It reminded her that impact didn't require wealth just intention. That moment planted a quiet but persistent seed. After years of telling herself she'd give "when things were more stable," she finally chose to act, even though life still wasn't as settled as she would've liked.

She started small, setting aside just 1% of her income each month, about $30 for charity. But she directed it toward causes that genuinely mattered to her: book drives for underserved students and local food banks providing essential meals. It wasn't a grand gesture. But it was hers.

To her surprise, that $30 didn't strain her finances at all. In fact, it did the opposite. Giving became a quiet source of strength and joy. What began as a small experiment became a steady rhythm one that added purpose to her spending, confidence to her decisions, and a deepening sense that she was part of something bigger than herself.

Creating a Giving Plan That Aligns With Your Values

Sporadic generosity can be heartfelt, but when your giving is aligned with your values and integrated into your financial life, it becomes something far more powerful: a consistent force for impact. Thoughtful, intentional giving ensures that your contributions are not just generous, but also meaningful and effective.

Steps to Intentional Giving:

- **Start with what truly matters to you.**

  Take time to reflect on the causes that stir something deep within you, education, healthcare, poverty alleviation, food security, the environment, or any other issue you care about. When your giving flows from genuine alignment with your values, it feels purposeful rather than pressured.

- **Choose your method of giving.**

  Not all generosity has to be financial. Time, skills, gently used goods, and even professional expertise can have powerful impact. You might volunteer at a local school, donate items to a shelter, or explore *impact investing*, where your money works for both financial and social returns.

- **Make giving part of your financial rhythm.**

  Decide on a specific percentage of your income to allocate, whether it's 1%, 3%, or 5%. Start with what feels realistic, and grow it over time. The consistency matters more than the amount. Just like saving, generosity becomes most transformative when it's built into your routine.

TRY THIS:

Choose a percentage of your income, say, 1%, and commit to giving it monthly to a cause you care about. Over time, increase this amount as your finances allow. You're not just donating; you're building a habit of intentional generosity.

HOW TO GIVE MORE AND GIVE SMARTER

Generosity doesn't require wealth. Even within a modest budget, there are creative, sustainable ways to make a meaningful difference. And when paired with intentional strategies, your giving can stretch further and create lasting impact.

Creative Ways to Give More:

- **Give your time or skills.**
  Volunteering can be just as powerful as financial giving. Whether you're tutoring, helping with logistics at a local event, or offering technical expertise, your time and effort are often exactly what nonprofits need most.
- **Use cashback and reward points.**
  Many credit cards and finance apps now allow you to donate accumulated points or cashback directly to charitable organizations. It's a simple way to give without dipping into your bank account.
- **Tap into employer matching.**
  Some workplaces match donations made by employees, sometimes even doubling them. If your company offers this benefit, it's an easy way to stretch your impact.
- **Support mission-driven businesses.**
  From brands that fund clean water projects to companies that donate a portion of profits, you can align your purchases with your values. Buying from these businesses lets you contribute without changing your overall spending.

TRY THIS:

This week, find one non-monetary way to support a cause you care about, whether it's donating unused items, offering your time, or simply choosing where you spend your money more thoughtfully.

ENSURING YOUR DONATIONS MAKE AN IMPACT

Not all charities are created equal. While many operate with noble intentions, some are far more effective than others at turning donations into real, lasting outcomes. That's why thoughtful giving begins with thoughtful research.

Before donating, take time to examine an organization's transparency and track record. Look into how it allocates funds what percentage goes directly to programs versus administrative costs and whether it reports measurable results. Tools like Charity Navigator, Give Well, and Charity Watch can help guide this process, offering insight into how efficiently and effectively different nonprofits operate.

Whenever possible, prioritize high-impact organizations, those that not only state clear goals but also demonstrate meaningful progress. Whether it's lives improved, communities served, or specific challenges addressed, these groups provide tangible evidence of their impact. That clarity helps ensure your contribution is doing the most good it can.

Finally, consistency matters. Rather than giving only in response to appeals or emergencies, consider setting up regular contributions to the causes you care about. Even small, recurring donations can have a greater cumulative impact than sporadic, one-time gifts. Steady support allows nonprofits to plan ahead, allocate resources more effectively, and sustain their work throughout the year.

TRY THIS:

Before your next donation, choose one organization and spend five minutes reviewing its impact. A little intention can go a long way toward making sure your generosity truly counts.

Strategies for Maximizing Impact

Giving isn't limited to writing checks it can take many forms, especially when approached strategically. To make the most of your generosity, consider going beyond individual donations and exploring broader, more impactful methods of contribution.

One powerful approach is collaborative giving. By joining forces with friends, family, or colleagues who care about the same cause, you can pool resources to create a greater collective impact than you might achieve alone. Whether through a formal giving circle or an informal shared effort, collective generosity amplifies results and fosters a sense of shared purpose.

Another strategy is to use your voice, not just your wallet. Advocacy and awareness-building can significantly expand the reach of your support. When you speak up about a cause, please share it with your network, or encourage others to get involved. You create a ripple effect inviting curiosity, sparking dialogue, and potentially inspiring others to give, too.

You can also align your investments with your values. Through impact investing, you direct your money toward ventures that aim to deliver both financial returns and measurable positive outcomes such as clean energy, affordable housing, or microloans for underserved entrepreneurs. It's a way to let your capital serve the world as well as your portfolio.

By thinking strategically through collaboration, advocacy, and values-aligned investing you can turn generosity into a force multiplier, extending your impact and deepening your sense of purpose over time.

FINAL CHALLENGE: THE 30-DAY GIVING WITH PURPOSE PLAN

To help you integrate intentional giving into your life, here's a 30-day challenge designed to make generosity both fulfilling and sustainable.

- *Choose a cause that resonates with you:* select a cause that aligns with your values and passions. It could range from supporting local food banks to funding clean water initiatives in developing countries.
- *Set aside a small amount for giving:* even a modest contribution, such as $5-10, can make a meaningful impact. The goal is to cultivate a habit of giving, regardless of the amount.
- *Please find a way to give that aligns with your strengths:* whether it's donating money, volunteering your time, or supporting a mission-driven business, choose a method of giving that feels authentic and sustainable for you.

Your Goal: By the end of the 30 days, you will have established a routine of intentional giving that enhances both your financial life and your sense of purpose.

CLOSING THOUGHTS: TRUE WEALTH INCLUDES GENEROSITY

Giving with purpose is one of the most powerful ways to align your money with your values. It transforms generosity from a passive obligation into an intentional practice one that enriches your life as much as it benefits others. When done with clarity and heart, giving becomes more than a reflection of what matters to you; it becomes a quiet signal of your growing financial confidence.

By creating a giving plan, exploring creative ways to contribute, and supporting causes that drive real change, you turn generosity into a cornerstone of your financial life. Giving doesn't weaken your stability; it reinforces your identity. Every act of contribution, whether through money, time, or attention, deepens your sense of meaning and connection. That's the lasting power of intentional generosity.

YOUR NEXT STEP:

Choose one cause that truly resonates with you, and take a small, meaningful action to support it today. Build the habit of purposeful giving, and let it transform you as much as it helps others.

What's Next?

In Chapter 13, we'll explore how the people around you can shape your financial journey for better or worse. From mentors to accountability partners, your financial community plays a powerful role in how confidently and consistently you move forward. You'll learn how to intentionally build a network that supports, challenges, and uplifts you as you pursue your goals.

The Strength of Shared Goals – Finding Your Financial Tribe

WHY COMMUNITY MATTERS IN FINANCIAL SUCCESS

Money is often seen as a solo pursuit, a quiet journey navigated through spreadsheets, podcasts, and late-night budgeting sessions. But in reality, financial well-being is rarely built in isolation. It grows stronger and more sustainable when shared.

For years, Noah believed money was something you figured out on your own. He read the finance books. He listened to the podcasts. He fine-tuned every detail of his budget. But he never talked about it. When friends brought up money, he stayed quiet. When he hit a roadblock, he kept it to himself. "I'll figure it out," he always thought. It wasn't until he joined a small financial support group that he realized what he'd been missing. Managing money alone, he discovered, isn't just lonely, it's limiting.

Your financial ecosystem, the attitudes, conversations, and habits modeled by those around you, shapes your trajectory more than you realize. If everyone in your circle is winging it, living paycheck to paycheck, those patterns quietly become your baseline. But when you're surrounded by people who are intentional, informed, and committed to long-term growth, your entire mindset shifts. In a strong financial tribe, wealth-building stops feeling abstract. It starts to feel normal.

The Isolation Trap

Like Noah, most people try to manage their finances alone. It's understandable, money remains a deeply personal and often taboo topic in many cultures, wrapped in secrecy and shame. People hesitate to share their struggles, goals, or successes, fearing judgment or unwanted comparison. But silence comes at a cost.

When you're isolated, motivation can quietly erode. Someone saving aggressively for a down payment might lose steam after a few setbacks not because the goal is impossible, but because there's no one to encourage them, offer fresh ideas, or remind them why it matters. Decision-making becomes harder without outside perspective. You might avoid investing entirely because no one in your circle does, or you might rush into buying a car you can't truly afford, simply because no one challenged your thinking. Without a network of trusted voices, it's easy to feel overwhelmed, stuck, or even defeated. Financial isolation doesn't just slow your progress it shrinks your vision of what's possible and makes financial growth feel heavier than it needs to be.

The Power of Connection

Fortunately, the antidote to financial isolation is simple but transformative: connection. Surrounding yourself with a supportive financial community makes building wealth not only more achievable, but more meaningful. When you share your financial journey including your goals, obstacles, and wins with people who understand and support you, something shifts. You gain momentum.

Mutual accountability keeps you focused. Shared inspiration lifts your energy when progress feels slow. And the collective wisdom of others, especially those who've faced similar challenges can offer insights you might never discover on your own. A financial tribe doesn't just cheer you on; it sharpens your thinking, expands your options, and makes the path far less lonely.

In this chapter, you'll learn how to find and connect with the right financial tribe to accelerate your growth. We'll explore the mechanics of accountability, how to build a network aligned with your goals, the power of mastermind groups, and the strength of mentorship. By the end, you'll have a clear path to creating a financial community that lifts you as you rise.

THE POWER OF FINANCIAL ACCOUNTABILITY

Accountability is one of the most effective tools for achieving any meaningful goal, and your finances are no exception. When you're accountable to someone else, you're far more likely to follow through on your commitments, stay motivated, and make thoughtful decisions.

Financial accountability is often underrated, but it can be transformative. It helps you stay focused when everyday distractions threaten to blur your long-term priorities. A trusted accountability partner or group offers consistent check-ins that keep your deeper "why" front and center, reinforcing your goals and sustaining your momentum.

It also acts as a safeguard against costly missteps. Talking through major decisions like a significant purchase or new investment with someone you trust invites perspective. That extra pause for reflection can help you avoid impulsive choices or risky moves you might later regret.

Even on a smaller scale, accountability shapes your daily habits. Just knowing someone will ask how it's going adds a gentle layer of awareness. You're more likely to spend mindfully, save intentionally, and stick to your plan because you've committed out loud.

And perhaps most importantly, accountability becomes a lifeline during hard times. Everyone hits roadblocks. But when you face them alongside someone who gets it, the weight feels lighter. Whether it's encouragement, perspective, or simply the reminder that you're not alone, that kind of support can mean the difference between giving up and pressing forward with renewed strength.

STRATEGIES TO ENHANCE FINANCIAL ACCOUNTABILITY

To fully unlock the benefits of accountability, it helps to approach it with intention and structure. The first step is setting clear, specific financial goals ideally before inviting an accountability partner into the process. Whether you're saving for a home, paying off debt, or building an investment portfolio, clarity creates direction. It gives both you and your partner a roadmap to follow. Without it, tracking progress becomes difficult, and motivation can start to fade.

Technology can also be a powerful ally. Apps like YNAB or Mint allow you to monitor your spending and savings in real time, giving you a clear picture of how you're tracking against your goals. Sharing snapshots or insights from these tools with your accountability partner creates objective check-in points and sparks more focused, productive conversations.

Equally important is celebrating progress along the way. Even small milestones deserve recognition. Whether it's paying off a credit card or hitting your monthly savings target, pausing to celebrate reinforces momentum and strengthens your connection to the process.

But most of all, embrace transparency. It's easy to share the wins; it takes courage to share the setbacks. True accountability is built on honesty. When you're open about missed goals or tough moments, you invite deeper support, empathy, perspective, and the encouragement to keep going. That kind of trust transforms accountability from a simple check-in into a powerful, lasting source of motivation.

Noah's Turning Point:

For a long time, Noah's financial goals lived quietly in his head. He meant well, he read books, listened to podcasts, and genuinely wanted to improve. But despite his sincere intentions, his goals remained vague. He believed he was being proactive, but without realizing it, he lacked structure, timelines, and accountability. These were his blind spots.

Everything shifted when he joined a financial peer group.

There, Noah learned the power of setting specific, trackable targets. He stood up and committed out loud, in front of others, to saving $5,000 for an emergency fund. It was a goal he'd quietly chased for years. But speaking gave the goal weight. Sharing it made it real. And knowing others were listening gave it urgency the kind of momentum he'd never quite found on his own.

The real transformation came through rhythm. Every two weeks, the group met to check in. They shared progress, exchanged strategies, and leaned on each other's experiences. That consistency didn't just bring structure and clarity. It sparked something deeper: energy and belief. Noah stopped feeling like he had to figure everything out alone.

The result? He reached his $5,000 goal months ahead of schedule. Not because he earned more or slashed his spending, but because, for the first time, he wasn't doing it alone.

TRY THIS:

Identify someone in your life who shares a similar financial mindset or goal whether it's saving, budgeting, or investing and invite them to be your accountability partner. This could be a trusted friend, a family member, or even a colleague. Set a regular rhythm to check in weekly or monthly and use those conversations to celebrate progress, troubleshoot setbacks, and outline your next steps. Over time, these consistent check-ins won't just keep you on track they'll build quiet momentum that compounds in powerful ways.

HOW TO BUILD YOUR FINANCIAL NETWORK

Building a strong financial network doesn't happen overnight but the effort pays off in lasting, meaningful ways. A supportive community can offer encouragement, fresh insights, and opportunities you might never uncover on your own. The key is to be intentional not only about *finding* the right people, but also about *how* you engage with them.

A great place to begin is online. Platforms like LinkedIn, Facebook, X (formerly Twitter), and niche forums host countless communities focused on budgeting, investing, financial independence, or entrepreneurship. But don't just scroll, join the conversation. Follow thought leaders, comment thoughtfully, ask questions, and share your own reflections when you can. Real engagement helps you find your voice and signals to others that you're serious about growth.

Outside of digital spaces, live events can be game changers. Webinars, finance workshops, local meetups, and investing clubs are not only educational, they're rich with networking potential. Attending even one in-person event can spark conversations that lead to lasting connections. Sometimes, asking a smart question during a Q&A or chatting with someone after a session leads to deeper relationships than any social media interaction ever could.

At a personal level, one of the most underrated strategies is starting financial conversations with people you already know. With trusted friends, family, or colleagues, gently open the door to money topics. Instead of diving into exact numbers, talk about goals, strategies, or challenges. Many people want to talk about money, but they're waiting for someone else to go first. When done respectfully, these conversations can reveal shared goals, spark new ideas, and even lead to accountability partnerships.

Mentorship is another powerful way to grow your financial network. Learn from mentors and experts by engaging with their books, podcasts, blogs, or online courses and don't hesitate to reach out if they offer coaching or community interaction. Following just a few seasoned voices can sharpen your thinking and accelerate your progress.

Volunteering is another path worth considering. Offering your time or skills to financial literacy programs or community education efforts not only helps others, it also connects you with people who care about the same things you do. Shared purpose often builds the strongest bonds.

Finally, if you feel inclined, consider sharing your journey. Whether through a blog, podcast, or even short social media posts, being open about your financial path can attract like-minded people to you. You don't have to be an expert. Sometimes, simply being honest about where you are invites others to walk alongside you.

The financial world doesn't have to be a lonely one. With curiosity, courage, and consistency, you can build a tribe that not only supports your goals but helps you reach them faster.

Noah's Shift: From Quiet Effort to Collaborative Growth

Noah's financial transformation didn't stop with hitting his emergency fund goal. Once he experienced the power of accountability, his mindset began to shift in deeper ways. He realized he didn't just need someone to check in with he needed a *community* that talked about money the way he wanted to: openly, curiously, and without shame.

So he widened his circle. He joined an online investing group where long-term strategies and wealth-building ideas were discussed freely. He began following financial mentors whose values aligned with his own, commenting thoughtfully and even engaging in direct conversations. Slowly, he started weaving money into casual conversations with close friends something he'd never dared to do before. To his surprise, many of them welcomed the topic, grateful for a chance to speak about their own financial journeys without fear of judgment.

Where he once felt alone, he now felt connected. Where he once kept his goals hidden, he now found shared ambition. And through this growing web of relationships, Noah didn't just learn more, he became more confident, more proactive, and more willing to reach for goals he'd never have dared to pursue on his own.

TRY THIS:

Find and join one online or in-person financial community this week, whether it's a budgeting group, an investing forum, or a local finance meetup. Don't just observe; introduce yourself, ask a question, or share a small part of your journey. The goal is participation. Real growth often begins with a single connection.

Financial Peer Support Groups – The Power of Collective learning

A financial peer support group is a small, focused circle of like-minded individuals who meet regularly to talk about money, set personal goals, and hold each other accountable. These groups blend the strengths of accountability, peer learning, and shared wisdom, creating a powerful structure for sustainable financial growth.

To start or join a group like this, begin by gathering three to five people who are genuinely committed to improving their finances. Look for members who not only share your seriousness and values but also bring a mix of experiences to the table. Diversity in background can enrich discussions, spark new ideas, and create a more well-rounded learning environment.

Once your group is formed, establish a consistent meeting rhythm. Whether you connect weekly, biweekly, or monthly, regular check-ins help maintain momentum and build trust. Over time, these meetings become an anchor keeping everyone on track, fostering reflection, and preventing drift.

During your sessions, explore a wide range of topics relevant to the group. From budgeting and saving to investing, debt management, or even career and income strategies, allow the conversations to evolve naturally while staying grounded in each member's real-life journey. Honest dialogue about both wins and setbacks is what makes these sessions truly transformative.

Most importantly, prioritize clear goal setting and mutual accountability. Each person should define a specific, measurable goal they're actively working toward. Dedicate time in each meeting for updates, sharing obstacles, and offering support. The power of the group doesn't come from perfection, but from consistent reflection, encouragement, and shared momentum.

Noah's Financial Peer Support Experience:

Within his peer support group, Noah set out to tackle a long-standing challenge: consistently increasing his investment contributions. He committed to a clear target to boost them by

20%. But the real breakthrough wasn't just setting the goal; it was how the group helped him think differently.

In their regular discussions, the group didn't just offer encouragement they questioned his assumptions. For instance, when Noah said he couldn't cut expenses without sacrificing his quality of life, someone asked him to walk through his last month of discretionary spending. That simple exercise uncovered habits he had overlooked: premium app subscriptions he rarely used, weekly takeout he had come to see as routine, and impulse Amazon purchases that added little real value.

Armed with this new perspective, Noah made deliberate changes. He canceled unused subscriptions, automated his investment transfers to occur right after payday, and adjusted his budget to better reflect what truly mattered. The result? He didn't just reach his target he surpassed it, increasing his investment rate by 25% in just three months.

The group didn't just keep him accountable. They sharpened his awareness, challenged his blind spots, and ultimately expanded what he believed was possible.

TRY THIS:

Think of 2–3 people in your circle who are also working toward better financial habits, maybe friends, colleagues, or even online connections. Reach out and suggest a trial meetup to share your goals, compare strategies, and explore whether a regular support group could help you all stay on track. Just one good conversation can be the start of something powerful.

MAKING YOUR FINANCIAL PEER GROUP EFFECTIVE

A peer support group is only as strong as the trust, structure, and energy that fuel it. To make yours truly effective, it's important to lay a solid foundation early on. Start by agreeing on a few core ground rules: active participation, confidentiality, and mutual respect. These aren't just formalities they create a safe space where members feel comfortable being open and honest.

It also helps to be mindful of the group's tone. While it's natural to admire someone's financial wins, the focus should remain on celebrating personal progress, not comparing outcomes. The goal is to uplift, not compete.

To keep things fresh and inclusive, consider rotating leadership within the group. Let different members take turns guiding discussions or sharing insights on topics they've explored. This shared responsibility brings in new perspectives and prevents the group from leaning too heavily on any one voice.

You might also invite occasional guests. Whether it's someone who's built a successful side hustle, a tax expert, or an investor with practical strategies, bringing in outside voices can deepen the group's learning and spark new ideas.

And finally don't just talk, track. Use a shared document or simple app to log goals, milestones, and progress updates. Seeing each other's efforts documented over time adds a powerful layer of accountability and reinforces the sense that everyone is moving forward together.

Learning From Others – Mentorship & Peer Influence

One of the fastest ways to accelerate your financial growth is to surround yourself with people who are already further along the path. Whether it's a mentor, a peer, or even someone you quietly observe, their experiences can become stepping stones for your own.

Start by identifying individuals whose financial habits or life decisions you genuinely admire. A mentor doesn't need to be a formal advisor they might be a friend, relative, manager, or even someone you follow online. What matters is that they've walked the road you hope to take. Their insights especially the ones forged through mistakes and hard-earned wins can help you navigate your journey with more confidence and clarity.

You don't always need direct access to learn. Some of the most powerful lessons come from close observation. How do financially stable people manage their time? What habits do they maintain? How do they make decisions when resources are limited or priorities collide? Quietly paying attention can uncover patterns worth emulating.

And when you do get the chance to ask for advice, take it. Most people are more generous with their knowledge than you might expect, especially when approached with sincerity and respect. Be concise. Be specific. Show that you've done your homework. Ask thoughtful questions, and always follow up with a genuine thank-you. Gratitude builds relationships more reliably than any tactic or networking script.

Perhaps the most overlooked part of learning from others is being open to honest feedback. Not every suggestion will be easy to hear, but a willingness to reflect, adjust, and apply what you've learned is what turns good advice into lasting transformation.

Eventually, your growth will create an opportunity to give back. Someone else will be looking for guidance, just as you once were. Don't hesitate to share your lessons. Mentoring others doesn't just reinforce what you know; it strengthens the kind of financial ecosystem where everyone rises together.

TRY THIS:

Think of one person whose financial habits, mindset, or results you truly admire. It could be someone in your personal circle, a colleague, or even a local entrepreneur. Reach out with a brief, respectful message asking for a few minutes of their time. Be specific about what you hope to learn and how their perspective could help you. Sometimes, one thoughtful question is all it takes to spark a conversation that shifts your path entirely.

FINAL CHALLENGE: THE 30-DAY FINANCIAL TRIBE EXPERIMENT

For the next 30 days, challenge yourself to:

1. **Connect with at least one person who shares your financial goals:** This could be a friend, colleague, or someone you meet in a financial community.
2. **Join one financial group (online or in-person):** Engage actively by participating in discussions, asking questions, and sharing your experiences.
3. **Set up regular accountability check-ins with a financial partner:** Use these meetings to track your progress, discuss challenges, and celebrate wins.

Your Goal: Surround yourself with people who push you toward financial success. By the end of the 30 days, you should feel more motivated, supported, and confident in your financial journey.

CLOSING THOUGHTS: YOUR ENVIRONMENT SHAPES YOUR WEALTH

Financial success is rarely achieved alone. Ambitious goals become more attainable and more fulfilling when pursued within a supportive, growth-minded community. The people around you shape your habits, influence your decisions, and ultimately impact your outcomes.

By intentionally curating that environment, your financial tribe becomes a source of energy, accountability, and resilience. You learn from those ahead of you, grow alongside peers, and stay connected to a vision that's bigger than your own.

YOUR NEXT STEP:

Choose one small action today. Join a group, reach out to a mentor, or ask someone to be your accountability partner. The earlier you begin building your financial tribe, the sooner you will start to see lasting results.

What's Next?

In Chapter 14, we'll take a step back to ask a deeper question: *What does wealth really mean?* Beyond numbers and net worth, true success includes balance, purpose, and fulfillment. We'll explore how to define financial freedom on your terms, and how to build a life that feels as rich as it looks.

Redefining Wealth – What Success Really Means

MORE THAN JUST MONEY

For most of her life, Emma believed she was doing everything right. She'd followed the formula everyone around her seemed to trust: study hard, land the right job, climb the ladder. And her diligence paid off. By her early thirties, she had the corner office, a generous salary, and a lifestyle that looked enviable from the outside. Her apartment was sleek and immaculate, the kind of space guests called "goals." She didn't just have nice things. She had, by most standards, arrived.

But the satisfaction she expected never quite settled in. On paper, everything was in place. In reality, her days blurred into a cycle of deadlines and back-to-back meetings. The skyline outside her window was breathtaking, yet she rarely paused long enough to admire it. Her calendar was full, but her life felt oddly hollow.

The more she achieved, the smaller her world seemed to become. The promotions, the bonuses, the accolades they stacked up, but not in the way she'd imagined. She was earning more than ever, yet she couldn't recall the last time she had dinner with her parents or spent a weekend without checking her email. Her friends stopped inviting her out, not out of resentment, but because they already knew the answer. She kept telling herself it was temporary. That this was simply the price of ambition. But one evening, after another fourteen-hour day, she dropped her bag by the door, collapsed onto the couch in the stillness of her apartment, and a different thought rose to the surface. One that had been quietly waiting in the background, growing harder to ignore.

"Is this it?"

That question changed everything. Not because she had failed but because she had succeeded, and still felt lost. In that moment of honesty, something shifted. She began to see her life more clearly, not as a series of accomplishments, but as a reflection of priorities she had never fully chosen. The world she'd built impressive, polished, enviable had been shaped more by external expectations than by her values.

It wasn't that money didn't matter. It had opened doors she never thought she'd walk through, funded comforts her parents once only dreamed of. But for Emma, it had stopped meaning something. Because no matter how high the numbers climbed, they couldn't buy back what she was quietly losing: time, connection, energy, peace. Real wealth, she began to realize, wasn't a figure in a bank account. It was deeper, quieter. It was about how fully you lived, not just how much you earned. It was about waking up and feeling alive inside your own life.

WHEN THE DREAM STOPS FEELING RIGHT

From a young age, many of us are handed a simple formula: work hard, earn as much as possible, rise through the ranks. Quickly, we learn that money becomes the measure. Titles and promotions become the proof that we've arrived, that we're becoming who we were meant to be. And for a while, it feels like a kind of arrival. The progress is real. So is the praise. We start to believe in the story we've been given because, in the beginning, it rewards us. So we aim higher. Move faster. Learn to dress the part and speak the language of success. To friends and family, it looks like winning. It *sounds* like winning.

But somewhere along the way, something subtle begins to fracture. We stop calling home as often. We put off the trip. Cancel the dinner. We tell ourselves it's just a season, that it's worth it. That we'll rest later. But "later" keeps moving. Then one day, we realize we've started trading things we never meant to give up: time with people we love, the steadiness of our health, the peace that comes from not being pulled in ten directions at once.

And still, we keep going. Because the world keeps applauding. It keeps rewarding this version of success, the visible one, the quantifiable one, the kind you can screenshot and post. The one that looks good on paper, even when it feels hollow in private. We hesitate to question it, afraid we'll seem ungrateful or worse, like we're failing at the very thing we worked so hard to achieve.

But the disconnection doesn't go away. It grows. The longer we ignore it, the heavier it gets. Eventually, that quiet voice, the one that whispers *this isn't it,* starts getting louder. It shows up at night, in the middle of what should be rest. It shows up in meetings, on the train ride home, in the quiet spaces between milestones. And when we finally pause long enough to listen, we're often met with a sobering truth: We've built a life that looks right... but doesn't feel right.

This is the danger of chasing success as it's commonly sold. Not because money or achievement are wrong but because when they become the only compass, we lose sight of the things that once gave us direction. And by the time we realize it, we may have spent years postponing what actually matters.

We delay the dreams that once made us feel alive. We put relationships on hold, trusting they'll wait. We quiet the parts of ourselves that ask the harder questions the inconvenient ones. Eventually, those parts stop asking. They start grieving.

So the real question the one that cuts through all of it is this:

What are we chasing, and what are we giving up to catch it?

A Richer Definition

True wealth is a life that feels aligned from the inside out. It's the freedom to choose how you spend your time and the presence to truly enjoy it. It's waking up with clarity, knowing your days reflect what matters most. It's feeling well not just financially, but emotionally, relationally, and mentally. When your priorities shape your calendar, when peace isn't postponed, when your work supports your life instead of consuming it that's wealth.

This chapter is about reclaiming that definition. It's an invitation to pause, reflect, and reimagine what success truly means to you on your terms, and in your season. By the end, you won't just walk away with a new idea of wealth. You'll carry a clearer vision for the life you want to build and the steps to start moving toward it.

EXPANDING THE DEFINITION OF WEALTH

Real wealth is the steady feeling that your life reflects what matters most to you.

When we broaden our view of wealth beyond money, we begin to see a richer, more meaningful picture, one that includes five essential dimensions:

1. Time Freedom

Of all the currencies available to us, time is the most non-renewable. True wealth means having ownership over your hours so you're not always running, reacting, or recovering. It's the freedom to linger over breakfast, to answer when a friend calls, to pause the grind and say, *"Yes, let's go."* It's the quiet power of knowing your life isn't constantly being borrowed by someone else's agenda.

2. Health and Well-Being

No amount of financial success can compensate for poor mental, emotional, or physical health. Energy is the engine behind everything else. It's what allows you to be present, to focus, to laugh, to heal. When you're well mentally, physically, and emotionally, you're truly available for your own life. You can pursue goals without burning out. You can show up for others without running on fumes.

A wealthy life makes room for rest without guilt, movement without pressure, and care without waiting for a crisis.

3. Relationships and Community

Meaningful connection to be seen, supported, and loved is an irreplaceable form of richness. The people in your corner, the ones who know your story and show up in the quiet moments, aren't a footnote to success they're its foundation. Health is dinners that turn into late-night conversations. It's having the space to show up for others when it matters most and letting them do the same for you. Supportive friendships, strong family ties, and a deep sense of belonging can carry us through life's hardest seasons and amplify its brightest ones. Unlike money, love and trust can't be stockpiled they can only be nurtured.

4. Personal Growth and Purpose

To feel wealthy is to feel alive in your progress. Growth gives your days texture through work that matters, skills that stretch you, or causes that quietly call you forward. Purpose doesn't have to mean solving the world's biggest problems. Sometimes, it simply means doing something that feels honest. Something that uses you well. A wealthy life creates space for your gifts to meet the world. Because purpose is what makes effort feel meaningful, and without it, even the greatest material success can feel hollow.

5. Financial Stability

While money isn't the whole of wealth, it is often the soil where other forms of richness can take root. Financial security offers protection from chaos. It creates options the freedom to leave what's toxic, to pursue what's meaningful, or to simply rest. It's not just about abundance. It's about stability. The kind that allows you to build a life steady enough to hold what matters most.

Emma's Shift

Emma didn't quit her job or move to the countryside. Instead, she started with choices that seemed small, but felt meaningful. She moved her morning meetings back an hour so she could walk her kids to school. She scheduled one afternoon a week with no calls, no screens just time to read, cook, or rest. She unsubscribed from luxury brand newsletters and redirected that budget toward travel with friends she hadn't seen in years.

As her priorities shifted, so did her energy. Her calendar no longer reflected just her responsibilities, but what mattered most to her. Her definition of wealth evolved, shifting toward using her ambition to create a more complete, balanced life.

TRY THIS:

Take a moment to redefine wealth on your own terms. What does a truly rich life look like beyond just money? Write down your ideal vision, including how you'd spend your time, the quality of your health, the strength of your relationships, and the sense of purpose that would guide your days.

THE TRAP OF CHASING MONEY WITHOUT PURPOSE

After a certain point, more money doesn't change how we feel it only increases the figures we fixate on. The joy of a raise fades faster than expected. What once felt like security quickly turns into a new standard, then a new pressure. One promotion leads to the next income bracket, which leads to a bigger apartment, a better car, a higher-stakes lifestyle all while the underlying restlessness stays untouched.

We don't always notice the trap while we're in it. But there comes a moment maybe subtle, maybe sharp when you realize that despite earning more, you don't feel any freer. The work never ends, and the finish line keeps moving. And instead of using money as a tool to shape a life you love, it quietly starts defining you.

Signs You're Chasing Money Instead of Fulfillment

You might recognize this pattern if:

- Burnout persists, even with financial success. Income goals are met, savings grow, but energy is low, and joy is absent.
- Health and relationships are consistently sacrificed for work. Long hours, missed meals, and neglected connections begin to erode what money can't replace.
- Happiness remains flat, despite earning more. Raises bring brief satisfaction, followed by a return to restlessness. The finish line keeps moving.

TRY THIS:

Take a moment to reflect; are you chasing money as the end goal, or using it as a tool for freedom? Ask yourself: *If money were no longer a concern, how would I spend my time? What would I do differently starting today?* Let those answers guide your next financial decisions.

DESIGNING A LIFE THAT FEELS WEALTHY

Once you've redefined what wealth means to you, the next step is to start living in alignment with that vision, not someday, but right now. That process starts by asking a simple question: What kind of life do I actually want to live? For some, the answer might be more time with family. For others, it's the freedom to travel, to work on passion projects, open-ended time, or simply a morning that begins without urgency. Whatever your answer, naming those priorities becomes the compass that quietly guides everything else.

With that compass in hand, your money becomes a useful tool. You begin to notice how your spending habits reflect or contradict what you actually value. The impulse purchases, the expensive distractions, the things that once felt like improvements begin to look more like unnecessary turns. And slowly, without drama, you start redirecting those resources toward the life you truly want to build.

This is where your Life-Centered Budget returns as a practical guide to freedom. A way of choosing, again and again, to invest in what matters most.

Then comes something more subtle, but just as important. You start making space for joy now. Not later, once you've "made it." Not once you retire or hit a savings target. But now. In ordinary weeks, in imperfect seasons. You carve out time for the people, hobbies, and moments that make you feel fully alive. Because wealth isn't just about one big arrival, it's about a hundred small, rich moments you didn't postpone.

And through it all, you practice a quiet habit: gratitude. A grounded appreciation for what's already here. You begin to notice how much you already have, and how much of your wealth can't be measured in numbers. That awareness softens the grip of comparison, reduces the hunger for more, and helps you see that you're already living some part of the life you once hoped for.

This is the heart of wealth something you live into, decision by decision, with values at the center, and with the courage to define success on your terms.

TRY THIS:

Write down three things that make you feel truly rich, beyond money. These might be quiet moments with someone you love, time spent doing something creative, or simply a feeling of peace at the end of the day. Keep this list somewhere visible. Let it remind you that real wealth is often already within reach.

FINANCIAL SUCCESS AS A TOOL, NOT THE GOAL

Money is a powerful tool, and its real value shows when it begins to support a life that feels whole marked by freedom and meaning.

For Emma, the breakthrough came when she stopped asking how to earn more and started asking how much was enough to live well. That single question changed her relationship with money. She simplified her lifestyle and no longer spent to prove anything or to keep pace with others. Instead, she began directing her finances toward what truly mattered: time with her kids, space to think, and the freedom to choose how her days unfolded. Money became something she used, not something that used her.

That change in perspective was bold; it was about letting money support her values instead of defining her worth. And in doing so, she discovered a kind of wealth that couldn't be measured by income alone, but by how fully she was living.

Shifting the Money Mindset

1. Use money as a tool, not a scorecard. Let it serve your vision, whether that's travel, time with family, creative freedom, or supporting causes you care about.

2. Define "enough" on your terms. Let go of comparison. Focus instead on what you need to feel secure and fulfilled.

3. Prioritize freedom over status. Invest in experiences, well-being, and relationships, things that create a rich life from the inside out.

TRY THIS:

Define what "enough" means for you. How much money do you need to live life on your terms? Be specific about your financial goals and how they align with your vision of true wealth.

FINAL CHALLENGE: THE 30-DAY TRUE WEALTH EXPERIMENT

For the next 30 days, challenge yourself to:

- *Identify one area of life to improve:* choose one area (health, relationships, time) to focus on and take small, actionable steps to improve it.
- *Track your spending:* does your spending align with what matters most? Look for areas where you can cut back on unnecessary expenses and redirect that money toward your priorities.
- *Shift focus from money to well-being:* practice gratitude, prioritize self-care, and make time for the people and activities that bring you joy.

Your Goal: Start living a wealthier life today. True wealth is about creating a life that feels rich in every sense, and it's within your reach.

CLOSING THOUGHTS: REDEFINING SUCCESS ON YOUR TERMS

Success is about how fully you live, and real wealth begins when your finances, time, energy, and relationships start reflecting what truly matters to you. Money plays a role, yes, but it's only one part of a much deeper equation. Health, joy, purpose, and connection these are the forms of wealth that don't show up on a balance sheet, but shape the way life actually feels.

When you define wealth on your terms, you stop living by someone else's scoreboard. You begin shaping a life that reflects your priorities, let go of the need to prove yourself, and give yourself permission to live.

YOUR NEXT STEP:

Take one small action today that reflects your version of true wealth. Set a meaningful financial goal. Schedule time for rest or reflection. Call someone you care about. Every intentional step moves you closer to a richer life on your own terms.

What's Next?

In Chapter 15, we'll shift from reflection to action. You'll learn how to act on the clarity you've built, translating your vision into deliberate steps toward a life that feels expansive, intentional, and free.

Dare to Dream – Turning Bold Ideas Into Reality

WHEN DREAMS STAY DREAMS

Adrian was always full of ideas. Over coffee breaks and quiet evenings, he'd talk about launching his own company, backpacking through Southeast Asia, maybe even writing that novel he'd been sketching in his mind since college. His friends admired his energy. He had vision, and he spoke with conviction.

But nothing ever quite got off the ground. There was always a reason to wait a bit for more savings, one more course, another project to finish at work. And so, the ideas stayed in orbit. And the years passed. His dreams didn't vanish; they just sank quietly into the background, buried beneath responsibility and routine.

Then, one afternoon at a bookstore, of all places, he bumped into someone he hadn't seen in years: Daniel, a former colleague from his first job out of university. Daniel looked different, lighter somehow, less rushed and more certain. They sat by a window and caught up.

Daniel had done it. Left his job, started a consulting business, traveled to twelve countries, and published a travel memoir. He spoke with the ease of someone who had chosen the harder path and learned to live with it. Adrian smiled and nodded. He was happy for him. But something inside him ached. Daniel had reminded him of the version of himself that still lived in possibility, but had never taken shape in the real world.

That night, Adrian couldn't sleep. He lay awake asking himself a question he'd been avoiding for years: *What exactly am I still waiting for?*

The Real Reason We Don't Chase Our Dreams

Like Adrian, most people carry dreams. Some are vivid and well-defined, like launching a business, traveling the world, or writing a book. Others live quietly in the background, like a hope for more freedom, more meaning, more time, or simply pursuing a childhood passion. Dreams are the seeds of a fulfilling life often the earliest signs of a life we long to build. Yet for most people, these dreams remain just that: dreams. They never move beyond the realm of imagination, because the day-to-day has a way of drowning them out, the urgency of daily tasks, the weight of responsibility, and the quiet pressure to be practical. All of these create a kind of inertia that keeps so many of us from turning bold visions into real steps forward.

Beneath the surface, here are three of the most common reasons that hold us back the most:

1. Fear of failure or judgment.
Fear rarely arrives with full force. It tends to settle in quietly, shaping our thoughts with subtle questions: *What if I'm not good*

enough? What if this falls apart? What will people say? On the surface, it may feel like caution or maturity, but more often, it's a defense mechanism that keeps us still. Many people delay their dreams not because they lack ambition, but because they overrate how hard failure would be and underrate their ability to respond, recover, and grow from a setback. The fear of discomfort becomes larger than the promise of possibility.

2. Waiting for perfect conditions.

The idea of *"someday"* can be seductive. *I'll start when I've saved a bit more. I'll take the leap after this busy season.* "Just a little longer" becomes a comforting refrain. But life is never perfectly arranged for bold moves. The timing rarely feels perfect. And if we wait for the stars to align, the window to act can quietly close while you're still waiting. Starting before everything is in place is often better than not starting at all.

3. Lack of a clear action plan.

Dreams feel exciting until you try to turn them into a to-do list. But when we try to translate a dream into a sequence of real-world steps, uncertainty sets in. *Where do I start? What if I choose wrong?* The weight of figuring it all out at once can become overwhelming. And in that overwhelm, many people retreat not because the dream no longer matters, but because the path feels too vague to follow. Without a clear plan, even the most inspiring vision can feel distant and impossible. The weight of not knowing where to begin becomes its own reason to stop trying. But clarity doesn't always precede action. More often, it arrives after action has already begun.

And here's the truth: Success begins when you move forward despite your doubts, even when your hands are trembling and the path ahead is foggy, regardless of perfect confidence or complete readiness. You don't need to have everything figured out. You just need to take the first step and this chapter will help you do that.

IDENTIFYING YOUR BOLDEST DREAMS

What Makes a Dream Worth Pursuing?

Before a dream can be pursued, it must be recognized as worth the pursuit. Not every idea deserves your time, effort, or sacrifice. Some arise from passing moments like an Instagram post, a flash of envy, or a temporary fascination. They fade as quickly as they arrive. Others come from a deeper place. They tap into something enduring, echo your values, reflect your longings, and stir a sense of unfinished business in your life.

A dream worth pursuing ignites something within you. It excites you not just because of what you might achieve, but because of who you'll become along the way. It makes you feel more alive just by imagining it. Even if the path is long or uncertain, it feels meaningful. The idea of pursuing it pulls you forward, again and again.

These kinds of dreams often come with a quiet sense of risk. They stretch the limits of your current identity. They ask more of your courage, more of your discipline, more of your heart. And that's part of their purpose: genuine dreams require growth. They don't just move you forward; they call you deeper into yourself.

Another defining trait is alignment. A worthy dream feels internally resonant. It's not designed to impress others or validate expectations; it reflects your values from the inside out. If a dream feels like it's performing someone else's script, it won't last. But when it reflects your real priorities freedom, creativity, love, purpose, and meaningful contribution that's when it becomes sustainable. You return to it because it feels honest.

And yes, a dream that matters will often scare you. That fear is a sign that you're playing at the edge of what's familiar which is exactly where transformation begins. But fear is only part of the equation. If the anticipation outweighs the doubt if the vision still excites you after the nerves quiet down that's how you know you've found a dream that is both bold and right.

Adrian's Wake-Up Call

Later that evening, long after the bookstore lights had dimmed and the conversation with Daniel had ended, Adrian lay in bed, unable to sleep. The question came to him quietly at first, then louder: *What would my life look like if I had started five years ago?* He didn't need to answer it in full he already knew enough to feel the weight of it.

It wasn't that Daniel had been luckier, or more brilliant, or better connected. Adrian could admit that now, with a kind of exhausted honesty. The difference between them came down to one thing: Daniel had acted. While Adrian was gathering information, Daniel was gathering experience. While Adrian was waiting for clarity, Daniel was learning by doing. While Adrian was imagining, Daniel was building.

What stung was realizing how little time it had taken for someone else to change everything and how quickly the years had passed while he told himself the same familiar stories: *Not yet. Almost. Soon.*

That night, for the first time in a long while, Adrian stopped making excuses because the cost of waiting had finally become too high to ignore.

TRY THIS:
Write down your biggest dream, the one you'd pursue if absolutely nothing were holding you back. Don't edit or shrink it to make it realistic. Let your imagination run wild. What does it look like? How would it feel to be living it?

OVERCOMING FEAR & SELF-DOUBT

Fear and self-doubt are the most persistent enemies of bold dreams. They present themselves as realism, responsibility, and prudence. *"You're probably not ready." "Maybe this isn't the right time." "What if you try and it doesn't work?"* These thoughts rarely sound like fear; that's what makes them so persuasive. And if you listen closely, you'll notice a pattern: they don't offer clarity; they offer paralysis.

The hard truth is that fear doesn't vanish with more planning. It doesn't disappear once you reach a certain level of preparation or confidence. Fear stays. And if you're waiting for it to go away before you begin, you'll wait forever. The only way to move past it is to move with it to step forward, not because you feel fearless, but because the alternative is to remain stuck.

That shift begins by reframing what failure actually means. Most people treat it as a verdict, a final confirmation that they weren't meant for this. But failure is rarely final, and it's never as personal as it feels. As the saying goes, *"Failure is information."* A missed shot, yes, but also a hint about what to aim for next. People who succeed aren't the ones who avoid mistakes; they're the ones who learn faster, adjust quicker, and keep going when others stall out.

Big dreams feel paralyzing when viewed as a single mountain. But no one climbs Everest in one leap. So don't. Break it down. Focus on one small, useful step. What's the smallest, simplest action you can take today? Just do that. Then do it again tomorrow. Momentum isn't created by inspiration it's created by action, no matter how small.

And you don't have to do it alone. Dreams, especially bold ones, are hard to carry in isolation. Talk to people who've walked a similar path. Ask questions. Surround yourself with those who pull you forward. Seek out mentors, and connect with people already doing what you dream of doing. Or simply share your goals with someone who will cheer you on. Encouragement is a survival tool it reminds you of what you're capable of when doubt tightens its grip and your memory fails you.

Finally, train your mind to believe. Equip your imagination. Visualization is not wishful thinking, and it isn't just a trick for athletes it's a tool for anyone daring to do something hard. It's mental rehearsal. But do it with intent. Because here's the catch: the brain sometimes rewards imagined progress the same way it rewards real progress. Just picturing yourself writing the book, starting the business, or crossing the finish line can trigger a brief dopamine hit a feeling of satisfaction that makes action feel less urgent. You get the glow of the outcome without the effort of the path.

That's why your visualization must serve your actions not substitute for them. Don't imagine applause. Imagine persistence. See yourself navigating setbacks, staying focused, and showing up on the hard days. Self-confidence doesn't grow from daydreams it grows when your actions match your vision. The more your imagination connects to real steps you're taking, the more your future starts to feel real, not just imagined.

Adrian's Turning Point:

He didn't wait for the perfect moment anymore he made a decision to begin. That same week, he launched a barebones website for his business idea. He sat down and typed the opening paragraph of the book he'd carried in his head for years. He booked a one-way ticket to the first place on his travel list. And for the first time, his dreams felt less like fantasies and more like something already in motion.

TRY THIS:

Write down *one fear* that's been holding you back. Then, list a single action you could take despite that fear, something small enough to do today. If you're afraid of public speaking, you might spend five minutes practicing in front of a mirror. If you fear judgment, share a small part of your dream with someone you trust. The goal isn't to be fearless, it's to take action anyway.

Turning Ideas into Actionable Plans

It's easy to let a dream live in your head. Up there, it's safe, unchallenged, untested, and full of promise. It can't fail, it can't be judged, and it doesn't ask anything of you. But dreams that stay in your mind won't change your life. They hover *inspiring in theory, but inert in practice.*

To bring a dream into the real world, you need structure. Not a vague "let's see what happens" mindset, but a real plan one that moves your idea out of your imagination and into motion, step by concrete step. The goal is momentum. Because once you start moving, things become clearer, and your confidence begins to grow. Confidence doesn't come before you begin it comes because you began. Bold action starts with the courage to take that first step.

The Bold Action Plan

A bold action plan is exactly what it sounds like: a simple, practical way to move forward. Step-by-step movement. The goal isn't to perfect every detail, it's to make consistent progress. Here's how to start structuring your path:

1. Define your goal clearly and specifically.
Vague aspirations like "I want to be successful" lead to vague results. Instead, get precise. What are you actually trying to build or experience? "Launch a coaching business by December." "Write a 70,000-word novel in six months." "Save €10,000 to travel for a year." Specific goals sharpen your focus and give shape to your path.

2. Set a realistic timeline.
A deadline, even a self-imposed one, creates healthy urgency and gives structure to your progress. Break your goal into smaller milestones or checkpoints that track your progress. If your dream is writing a book, that might mean: research in August, outline by September, first draft by November. Realistic dates create rhythm and reduce overwhelm.

3. Identify your first, smallest action.
Start with one thing. The very first action might be as simple as researching three businesses in your niche, registering a domain name, or opening a document and writing the title. Think Minimum Viable Action. You need to act.

4. Make yourself accountable.
Don't rely on willpower alone. Tell someone you trust about your dream and your timeline. Choose someone who'll ask how it's going to support your follow-through. Whether it's a mentor, coach, friend, or peer group, outside accountability turns ideas into action and keeps momentum alive when motivation dips.

Adrian's Action Plan:

The spark had been lit weeks earlier when he launched that barebones website, wrote the opening paragraph of his book, and booked a one-way ticket. But now, Adrian knew momentum alone wouldn't be enough. It was time to get structured.

His vague ambition solidified into a clear goal: launch his online business within six months. The first milestone? Upgrade the site and publish a real offer by the end of the month. The second: land his first paying client within 90 days. That same week, he began studying three successful businesses in his niche, dissecting what actually worked.

But clarity didn't erase difficulty. The upgraded site took longer than expected. He second-guessed his pricing. One client ghosted him after a promising call. Still, each step gave him more traction. He stuck to the timeline, made adjustments where needed, and kept showing up. What made the difference was structure a clear goal, a defined timeline, a concrete next step, and just enough accountability to keep moving forward, even when things got messy.

> **TRY THIS:**
> Write down the very first action step you can take toward your dream, then do it today. Don't overthink it. Just take the first step.

BUILDING RESILIENCE & STAYING MOTIVATED

Every bold dream encounters resistance. You'll face setbacks, doubts will arise, and progress will stall. That's normal, it's the terrain. The difference between those who realize their vision and those who abandon it often comes down to one thing: resilience. The ability to keep going when motivation fades and the path gets hard.

How to Stay Motivated:

1. Celebrate small wins.
Don't wait for the finish line to acknowledge progress. Celebrate the first paragraph written, the first email sent, the first $100 saved. These moments might seem small, but they build belief and belief fuels momentum. Just as important: don't only celebrate outcomes; celebrate effort. Showing up and doing the work, especially when it's hard, is a victory in itself.

2. Adjust, don't quit.
Not everything will go as planned. Some strategies will fall flat. That's not failure it's feedback. Real progress demands flexibility.

So analyze, adapt, and keep moving. Obstacles don't mean you're on the wrong path; they mean you're on a real one.

3. Keep learning.

The bigger the dream, the more growth it demands. Whether it's reading, taking a course, finding a mentor, or practicing your craft, every act of learning builds competence and competence builds confidence. If you feel stuck, learning something new is often the fastest way to get unstuck.

4. Reconnect with your 'why.'

When things get tough, zoom out. Remind yourself why this dream mattered in the first place. What kind of life were you trying to build? What feelings were you chasing? Revisiting your original intention can reignite your purpose especially on the days when motivation is hard to find.

Adrian's Lessons in Resilience

Adrian's early momentum gave him a glimpse of what was possible, but real life didn't follow a clean trajectory. His first product launch flopped. The travels that were meant to inspire him left him drained. The book he'd been so excited to write stalled halfway through. But instead of treating those moments as proof he'd failed, he saw them as invitations to adapt.

He didn't scrap the business; he got curious. He listened more closely to what his audience actually needed and reshaped his offer. When constant travel left him exhausted, he stopped chasing places and slowed down, choosing depth over speed. And when publishers passed on his manuscript, he chose to self-publish on his terms. His dream didn't die when things got messy. It matured. Because resilience means staying in motion, learning as you go, and refusing to let temporary setbacks rewrite the bigger story.

TRY THIS:

Write a short letter to yourself about why your dream matters. Remind yourself of the vision, the purpose, and the feeling behind it. Keep it somewhere visible, read it whenever doubt creeps in or momentum fades. Let your own words pull you back to center.

FINAL CHALLENGE: THE 30-DAY BOLD ACTION CHALLENGE

For the next 30 days, challenge yourself to:

1. Take one action daily toward your dream.
2. Replace fear with action. When doubt creeps in, take a step anyway.
3. Track your progress and celebrate small wins.

Your Goal: Turn your boldest idea into reality by taking consistent action.

CLOSING THOUGHTS: YOUR DREAMS ARE WAITING FOR YOU

The life you imagine won't build itself. It depends on your willingness to begin to stay focused, to adjust, to persist, and to believe. No one else can step in and live it for you. The agency is yours.

Imperfect action beats perfect hesitation every time. What matters most isn't precision, it's motion. Progress over perfection. Direction over delay. And above all, the courage to begin again, especially when things get hard.

Because the only true failure is never daring to begin.

YOUR NEXT STEP:
Take one bold action today, even if it's small, and especially if it's small.

What's Next?

This is the final chapter, but your journey is just beginning. Step forward. Make it real. The life you've been dreaming of is waiting for you to claim it.

www.ingramcontent.com/pod-product-compliance
Lightning Source LLC
Chambersburg PA
CBHW021235130626
46554CB00004B/1508